Flourish

Flourish

A Visionary Garden in the American West

EDITED BY

Panayoti Kelaidis

DENVER BOTANIC GARDENS

JOHNSON BOOKS
BOULDER

Published by Johnson Books, a Big Earth Publishing company
1637 Pearl Street, Suite 201, Boulder, Colorado 80302
1-800-258-5830
E-mail: books@bigearthpublishing.com
www.bigearthpublishing.com

Cover and text design by Rebecca Finkel
Cover photo by Dan Johnson, Associate Director of Horticulture and Curator of Native Plants.
Cover illustration of Desert Beargrass by Linda Gerstle.

9   8   7   6   5   4   3   2   1

Library of Congress Cataloging-in-Publication Data
Flourish! A visionary garden in the American West / edited by Panayoti Kelaidis.
p. cm.
Includes index.
ISBN 978-1-55566-429-9
1. Denver Botanic Gardens—History.
2. Botanical gardens—Colorado—Denver—History.
I. Kelaidis, Panayoti. II. Title: 50 plants for 50 years.
III. Title: Celebrating fifty years of the York Street Denver Botanic Gardens.
QK73.U62D48 2009
580.73'78883—dc22
2008054624

Printed in China by Oceanic Graphic Printing

This book is gratefully dedicated to

Dr. Moras L. Shubert

Botanist, Gardener, Educator, and Friend

Professor Emeritus in Botany at the University of Denver

and Lifetime Board Member of Denver Botanic Gardens,

Dr. Shubert has served in a variety of capacities

on the Gardens' board from 1951 to present-day.

He has guided Denver Botanic Gardens

since its inception along with his wife, Erne.

Their constant and cheerful presence through the decades

has steadied our course and ensured our success.

Contents

Foreword by Brian Vogt ix

Acknowledgments xi

Introduction by Panayoti Kelaidis xiii

Denver Botanic Gardens' Historical Highlights 1

Early Visionaries 13

Plant Portraits 23

Photo Credits 144

Plant Index 145

Foreword

By *Brian Vogt*, Chief Executive Officer, Denver Botanic Gardens

LIFE, IN ITS DAZZLING VARIETY AND PURPOSES, fills our senses every day. Most of the time, we allow the sighting of a squirrel or the towering cottonwood next to the road to make only a minor dent in our consciousness. Life becomes a backdrop to our lives.

But every now and then we pause, absorb, and refresh ourselves with an interrelationship with life. When it comes to plants, it often takes numbers. An entire field of gold, a myriad of reddening leaves, or a hillside of synchronized grasses provokes a desire to snap a picture and stand in awe. But some plants can shine in solo performances. The single bloom of a waterlily in a still, black pool is an elegant sensation.

When we open our eyes at the right moment, plants connect to our DNA.

Back in 1959, a former cemetery began a new era as the Denver Botanic Gardens. For the next fifty years, thousands of individuals created a place where powerful and relevant connections could be made between people and plants. Among the Gardens' most important work is showcasing native species in ways that can make visitors see familiar friends in new ways. Science merging with art, nature with design, a fusion of forces reaches audiences to enlighten and enthrall.

We celebrate these fifty years with a selection of remarkable plants. Each has a story and each plays a part in a bigger story. The stewards who discovered, researched, cataloged, nurtured, and sustained these plants have done more than bring beauty to a special place. They have inspired gardeners. They have brought smiles to souls in need of healing, and wonder-filled gasps to children amazed at something they have never seen before.

Enjoy this chronicle of plants, of place and time. Most of all, enjoy the passion of so many who have ensured that when we stop for a moment to take stock of our surroundings, we are sure to appreciate the way the broad tapestry of life around us can transform and move us.

Acknowledgments

DENVER BOTANIC GARDENS has a long tradition in Botanical Art and Illustration. The discipline was first taught in 1980 and the certificate program was established in 1990. Today, the professional instructors continue this strong tradition, and the program offers a comprehensive education in the scientific illustration of plants and fungi, and the nearly one hundred courses in the traditional media: graphite, pen and ink, colored pencil, and watercolor are offered each year for students of all ages and at all levels of art experience. Comprehensive workshops in the more rare classical techniques such as silverpoint, egg tempera, and carbon dust, as well as modern methods of computer art, are frequently taught. The curriculum can lead to a Certificate in Botanical Art and Illustration, a recognition that is obtainable at only a few locations worldwide. In addition to students studying for certification, many others participate in the classes just for the joy of painting nature in all its beauty and detail.

Fifty of the more than four hundred active students in the program, as well as seven instructors, contributed the illustrations for this book.

—MERVI HJELMROOS-KOSKI, PH.D., D.SC.
Coordinator for Botanical Art & Illustration
Denver Botanic Gardens

MORE THAN ONE HUNDRED DEDICATED PEOPLE contributed to the development of this book. On behalf of Denver Botanic Gardens, I thank the many individuals in addition to the authors credited throughout the text who made the creation of this story possible and a great success. Deb Golanty of the Gardens' Helen Fowler Library deserves special credit for acting as a springboard for this entire effort. Her insight and organization were invaluable. Also within the library, thank-yous go to Colleen Nunn for photo captions and to volunteer archivist, Mary Lou Waldman, for seeking out the perfect historical photos to complement the timeline. For keen eyes during the editing process: Ann Berthe and Cindy Tejral-Newlander in the Gardens' Plant Records office. For plant identification for photography: Mike Kintgen and Lily Parra. Others provided much-needed photographs, including: Kirk Fieseler, Panayoti Kelaidis, Mike Kintgen, Lauren Springer Ogden, John Stewart, and Joe Tomocik. Thanks, too, to Barbara Baldwin for providing a photo of Carol Gossard. Kudos goes to Scott Dressel-Martin, the Gardens' official photographer, for maintaining a smile while under a remarkably tight deadline. Without the help of Mervi Hjelmroos-Koski, the botanical illustrations would not have come to be a reality. Finally, to Panayoti Kelaidis and Sarada Krishnan: sincere appreciation for developing the framework and identifying appropriate photographs.

—LISA M.W. ELDRED
Director of Exhibitions, Art & Library Collections
Denver Botanic Gardens

"Denver has great possibilities for developing something unique

among botanic gardens of America, or in fact, of the world.

Our high mountains, so near at hand, have a great variety

of climatic conditions, representing everything from here to the Arctic region.

With these mountains for growing cold-loving plants,

the units in the city for temperate zone plants, and the Conservatory

which is planned for this unit of the Gardens for growing tropical

and sub-tropical species, it will be possible to have in this vicinity

for study and exhibition a complete cross-section of the plant kingdom,

from the equator to the polar regions.

Few large cities of the world have this opportunity."

—DR. AUBREY C. HILDRETH
First director of Denver Botanic Gardens
speaking at the official dedication ceremonies of
Denver Botanic Gardens on Sunday, September 20, 1959

Introduction

By *Panayoti Kelaidis*

FIFTY YEARS AGO the Denver metropolitan area was quite different from what it is today. For one thing, only a fifth as many people lived along the Front Range: vacant lots filled with wildflowers were common in Boulder, where I grew up. Today, every last one of them boasts a megamansion. The toll road that connected Denver and Boulder passed through miles of prairie and farmland. Now only patches of open space remain between shopping centers and housing developments. I remember people complaining about the exorbitant toll of 25 cents on that road—which is about what most annuals, and even perennials—sold for. Horticulture in the Front Range, at the time when Denver Botanic Gardens' York Street site was first planted fifty years ago, would be unrecognizable to gardeners and nursery professionals today. Soil-less mixes, universal in nurseries today, were a novelty: plants used to be grown in (gasp!) soil! The assortment sold at garden centers would shock contemporary gardeners: no *Agastache*! No *Delosperma*! Nary a *Penstemon* to be seen for sale. The only salvia you might ever encounter in a nursery would have been *Salvia splendens*, the common red bedding plant that was used everywhere with dusty miller and marigolds, and nowadays has almost become an endangered species!

The late 1950s were a time of clean and green—junipers embellished with a few annuals (mostly petunias) grown from seed. We have witnessed a number of revolutions in horticulture over the last fifty years: the "perennial boom" began in the early 1980s. Perennials are still booming and here to stay. Ornamental grasses a few years later, along with the explosion of interest in dwarf conifers and exotic woody plants altogether: magnolias, Japanese maples, and more. The xeriscape movement was spurred by drought, but it also paralleled a fascination with native plants among cutting-edge gardeners. Container gardening has become the rage. Clean propagation media and tissue culture have hastened the sudden explosion of cultivars on the market to the extent that seed-grown plants (once the norm) are now almost the exception. All of these trends have happened more or less all over America, but they have all flourished in Denver with uncanny vigor. I believe the example of Denver Botanic Gardens has led the charge in transforming our urban and suburban landscapes in the past half century into far more beautiful, far more sophisticated spaces.

Over the past half century, the Gardens' horticulturists have tested tens of thousands of ornamental plants in a variety of garden settings. They have fanned out across America and abroad, visiting other botanic gardens and bringing back samples, seeking out plants in nature. These are studied through a veritable laboratory of processes outlined in the course of this book—grown in the greenhouses, observed, tested in a variety of sites, and finally displayed in the proper microclimate and context in one or more of the dozens of gardens that comprise Denver Botanic Gardens. In less than a decade a novelty like *Agastache rupestris* or the delospermas can go from tentative testing in the Rock Alpine Garden to being used in mass plantings on median strips throughout the metro area—indeed, across the globe. Such is the power of horticultural displays at the Gardens.

We have chosen distinctive plants to demonstrate the complexity and the fascinating stories that lie behind every one of the nearly 30,000 accessions that comprise the Gardens' collections at any given time. Gifted artists from Denver Botanic Gardens' Botanical Art & Illustration Program have painted each of these plants, and a cross section of staff members, volunteers, board members, and professionals in our community have researched and described these plants to provide testament to a magical moment in our horticultural and institutional history.

Many of these plants saw their horticultural birth, as it were, at the York Street site: *Scrophularia macrantha* had surely never before been grown in any garden before I collected a few capsules on Cooke Peak in Luna County, New Mexico, in 1992. This morning, on September 4, 2008, I saw dozens of specimens of this rare wild plant in the median strips and parks of Lakewood. *Penstemon strictus* 'Bandera' and *Penstemon digitalis* 'Husker Red' are native American wildflowers that have been improved and selected by horticultural researchers in New Mexico and Nebraska, respectively. Both penstemons are workhorses of American gardens today, and both were likely first displayed to the public at Denver Botanic Gardens. But this book also shows that plants in our collections, however beautiful and worthy, have sometimes quietly sat there, as it were, and seemingly languished. The miniature walnut of the southern Great Plains, *Juglans microcarpa*, will probably never become an important horticultural crop, to the enormous dismay of Denver's squirrel population no doubt. But this tree (and dozens more) are prized state Champion Tree specimens at York Street.

This book is a celebration of the horticultural renaissance that has occurred in the Rocky Mountain region in the past half century. It follows *Gardening with Altitude*, the first book designed, produced, and published by Denver Botanic Gardens' staff, in beginning to tell the story of the research efforts, the artistry of staff and volunteers, and the complexity of interactions responsible not only for collections at York Street, but in producing the very palette of plants that increasingly fill our garden centers, and in fact provide the very scenic backdrop of our lives from day to day in the city landscape.

Plant Select® is a well-known vehicle where novel plants from Denver Botanic Gardens and Colorado State University have found a ready market by the tens of millions. Long before Plant Select,® Denver Botanic Gardens was researching and distributing plants locally, and providing dramatic displays that modeled and publicized plants new to the industry. York Street has provided a setting for hundreds of weddings and concerts and magical moments as couples and horticultural students wander through its enchanted bowers. Dramatic exhibits of sculpture and art, symposia, and classes (and a never ending stream of school buses!) are just a few ways we reveal the magic of chlorophyll and nature to new generations.

I have always thought that botanic gardens were Cathedrals of Carbon, where people can acknowledge and honor the enormous debt that we owe the humble plant; after all, it is chlorophyll that produces the hydrocarbons that form the basis of all our very sustenance (aside from water, that is, and a dash of salt). Plants produce the oxygen we breathe and most of the fiber that clothes and houses us. Alas, it was fossil plants that captured the carbons that comprise petroleum, natural gas, and coal that are being released into the atmosphere by the metric ton every minute, which are in fact causing the potentially cataclysmic scenario that threatens the future of our planet. And it is in the power of plants to sequester carbon that proffers one avenue for reversing our fatal course.

This book, compiled by a hundred hands, is a primer of the dynamic process of art, science, and delight that we call Denver Botanic Gardens. If we can have accomplished so much in the infancy, as it were, of our first fifty years, I cannot begin to imagine the enormous potential for enlightenment, experimentation, and beauty that is possible in the fifty years to come.

Historical Highlights

Compiled by *Deb Golanty*; photo research by *Mary Lou Waldman*

1941

Kathryn Kalmbach presents a motion that the Colorado Forestry Association (CFA) "endorse and aid in the establishment of a Botanic Garden." The association had been formed on November 19, 1884. Among its many prominent members were Walter Cheesman and Henry M. Porter. Their daughters (Mrs. John Evans and Mrs. James J. Waring) were to become driving forces in the formation of a botanic garden for Denver.

Mrs. Kathryn Kalmbach.

1944

Gladys Cheesman (Mrs. John) Evans is elected president of CFHA. She generously provides a headquarters at 1355 Bannock Street, which became known as Horticulture House, and was eventually demolished to build Denver Art Museum.

First issue of *The Green Thumb News* is published under the editorship of George W. Kelly. It includes a seminal piece by Saco Rienk (S.R.) DeBoer titled, "The Colorado Landscape": *"The Colorado landscape ... is different. It dares the man from other states to understand it, to work with it successfully. It requires ... an understanding of the Landscape of the Rockies."*

Horticulture House.

1943

CFA merges with the Denver Society of Ornamental Horticulture to form the Colorado Forestry and Horticulture Association (CFHA), with Walter Pesman as president.

1949

In October, a Plant Auction is held to benefit CFHA.

Mrs. John Evans.

1951

Mr. and Mrs. John Evans finance a detailed plan, drawn by S.R. DeBoer, for a botanic gardens in City Park. The plan is accepted by the city, and the Botanical Gardens Foundation of Denver, Inc. is incorporated on February 3, 1951. The first meeting of the Foundation is held on February 27, 1951, at the home of Mr. and Mrs. Evans. Among the officers elected is Dr. Moras L. Shubert, secretary-treasurer.

Dr. Moras L. Shubert.

1952

S.R. DeBoer's plan for a fifteen-year, $1.5 million master plan is approved by the board and presented to Denver City Council, which designates 100 acres in the southeast corner of City Park for the Denver Botanical Gardens, as it was called then.

2

Site of an early incarnation of Denver Botanic Gardens.

1957

An Alpine Tundra Study Area is set aside on Mount Goliath, about 50 miles from Denver. Established by permission of the U.S. Forest Service and jointly maintained, the site consists of 160 acres, ranging in altitude from 11,500 to 12,150 feet, with a spectacular forest of bristlecone pine (*Pinus aristata* Engelm.). A two-mile trail is named in honor of Walter Pesman.

Mount Goliath Research Area.

1954

Robert Woerner, a landscape architect and horticulturist from Spokane, is selected by the trustees and the city to direct the Gardens full time, succeeding George Kelly.

1958

In response to vandalism problems at City Park, the Botanical Gardens Foundation of Denver considers development of an herbaceous unit on York Street.

Historic view of present site of the Gardens.

1959

Dr. and Mrs. James J. Waring transfer ownership of 909 York Street to Denver Botanic Gardens (designed in the 1920s by architect Jacques Benoit Benedict for the Richard Crawford Campbell family), adjacent to an 18-acre plot once occupied by Mt. Calvary Cemetery and now owned by the city.

Waring House, used for administrative functions, 909 York Street.

1960

In August, the Denver Botanic Gardens Guild is formed under the name of Denver Botanic Gardens Junior Committee and commits to a study of herbs and sponsorship of a model garden. ❧

In November, Scott Wilmore, president of CFHA, and Lawrence A. Long, president of the Gardens, jointly announce that the two organizations have merged. Ruth Porter (Mrs. John J.) Waring becomes vice president; John C. Mitchell, treasurer; and Anna R. (Mrs. George) Garrey, assistant secretary-treasurer of the Board. ❧

Lawrence A. Long and Scott Wilmore

1959 (continued)

Dr. Aubrey C. Hildreth, who had retired as director of the U.S. Department of Agriculture's Experimental Station at Cheyenne, Wyoming, becomes director of the Gardens and presides at the official dedication ceremonies at York Street on Sunday, September 20, 1959. ❧

Dr. Aubrey C. Hildreth.

1961

Following the death in 1960 of Charles C. Gates, planting begins in the Gates Montane Garden according to the design of S.R. DeBoer. The design replicates the landscape around the Gates' family home—the Chateau—in Bear Creek Canyon, which had also been designed by DeBoer. ❧

The Gardens' York Street site, previously a Catholic cemetery.

The iconic Boettcher Memorial Tropical Conservatory.

1964

Construction begins on the new conservatory—the only conservatory in America made entirely of concrete and Plexiglas panes, individually preformed to increase strength and to channel humidity to the sides of the conservatory so condensation would not drip on visitors. ❧

In September, the Associates of Denver Botanic Gardens is founded by Fran Morrison, president of Around the Seasons Club. "Dusty" Smith of the Denver Botanic Gardens Guild is the first president of the Associates. ❧

A gift shop is begun in the foyer of the Waring House. ❧

1962

Dr. Helen Zeiner becomes Honorary Curator of the Kathryn Kalmbach Herbarium, following the death of Mrs. Kalmbach. ❧

Dr. Helen Zeiner.

1963

On January 7, the Board of Trustees of the Boettcher Foundation announces a $600,000 grant for a conservatory at Denver Botanic Gardens. By year's end, the Gardens and the city accept plans by Victor Hornbein and Edward White, architects. Gerald H. Phipps, Inc. is awarded the contract for construction. ❧

1965

Ernest Bibee, conservatory superintendent, is hired from Missouri Botanical Gardens. More than 600 species and varieties of tropical plants are acquired. ❧

A traditional bow-knot garden designed by Persis M. Owen contains culinary and medicinal herbs and dye plants. ❧

Ernest Bibee.

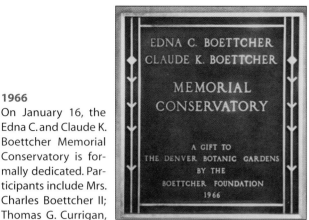

Boettcher Tropical Conservatory dedication sign, 1966.

1966

On January 16, the Edna C. and Claude K. Boettcher Memorial Conservatory is formally dedicated. Participants include Mrs. Charles Boettcher II; Thomas G. Currigan, mayor of Denver; John A. Love, governor of Colorado; Joe Ciancio, manager of Parks and Recreation; Lawrence A. Long, president of Denver Botanic Gardens; and Cris Dobbins, chairman of the Boettcher Foundation.

On August 29, Dr. Louis B. Martin, formerly of the Los Angeles County Department of Arboreta and Botanic Gardens, becomes director of Denver Botanic Gardens. He succeeds Dr. Hildreth, who retired with the title of Director Emeritus on August 31.

Dr. William G. Gambill, Jr. on left, Panayoti Kelaidis on right, 1980.

1970

In July, Dr. William G. Gambill, Jr. succeeds Dr. Martin as director of Denver Botanic Gardens.

In September, redevelopment of the Gardens is begun according to a plan prepared by Eckbo, Dean, Austin, and Williams, a leading firm of San Francisco landscape architects.

Construction of the pools, lakes, waterfalls, and fountains is begun by Langfur Construction, according to the engineering design of Wright-McLaughlin Engineers.

1967

Dr. D.H. Mitchel and Mary Hallock Wells move their mycology collections of native fungi species from the Denver Museum of Natural History to the Waring House, and Dr. Mitchel becomes Honorary curator.

1968

John C. Mitchell succeeds Lawrence A. Long as president of Denver Botanic Gardens' Board of Trustees.

John C. Mitchell.

1969

At a special meeting of the Board of Trustees on February 20, Hudson Moore Jr. announces an additional grant of $500,000 from the Boettcher Foundation for construction of an education building.

1971

In January, Solange Gignac is hired as the first staff librarian of the Gardens.

On March 6, the Education Building, "the newest addition to the Boettcher Memorial Complex," is presented by Cris Dobbins, board chairman of the Boettcher Foundation, to the city and county of Denver, with Mayor Bill McNichols accepting. In all, the Boettcher Foundation had granted $1.5 million to Denver Botanic Gardens. The building was designed by Hornbein and White, and added Horticulture Hall (now Mitchell Hall), a plant preparations room, the Helen Fowler Library, the Kathryn Kalmbach Herbarium and display area, the Lobby Court with its fountain and pool, and several other facilities.

Librarian Solange Gignac, 1982.

Denver Botanic Gardens at Chatfield.

Krohn House at 790 Gaylord Street, 1976.

6

1973

In March, Denver's city council authorizes Mayor Bill McNichols to sign a twenty-five-year lease on some 750 acres of land along Deer Creek near Chatfield Reservoir to be developed and maintained by Denver Botanic Gardens, acting in accordance with plans approved by the U.S. Army Corps of Engineers. ❧

Frieze depicting pioneers by sculptor Robert Garrison, 1926.

The walls in the Plains Garden are inset with the "Story of a Pikes Peaker," a 1926 frieze by Robert Garrison, which came to be known as the Covered Wagon Frieze, and ultimately, the Garrison Frieze. The plaques were originally sculpted for the Midland Savings Building in downtown Denver. ❧

Both the Boettcher Memorial Tropical Conservatory and the Waring House are designated landmarks for historical preservation. ❧

1976

David Krohn's house at 790 Gaylord Street, and most of its furnishings, are willed to Denver Botanic Gardens. The home was designed by Denver architect Ray Irwin and built in 1936. The will specified that "a house sitter" (either the Gardens' director or other personnel) live there for eight years, so Dr. Gambill took residence there in the spring. ❧

Denver Botanic Gardens begins to participate in an international seed exchange, Index Seminum. ❧

1974

In April, two new greenhouses are dedicated, more than doubling the capacity for growing plants. Funds were provided by the late Dr. John C. Long and the Associates. ❧

Anna's Overlook, named in honor of Mrs. Anna M. Garrey, "one of the pioneers in the establishment of Denver Botanic Gardens," is completed. ❧

Mrs. Anna M. Garrey.

1975

Under board President John C. Mitchell, a resolution is passed in honor of Mrs. Ruth Porter Waring. It designates "the Plains Garden as the Laura Smith Porter Plains Garden, designed by Jane Silverstein Ries, in honor of Mrs. Waring's mother, a pioneer citizen, who crossed the Great Plains to Denver in a covered wagon." ❧

Top: Mrs. Ruth P. Waring (right). Above: Laura Smith Porter Plains Garden.

1977

In June, the board votes to retain Professor Koichi Kawana to design and supervise construction of a Japanese Garden. Kawana is principal architectural associate and lecturer in Japanese art, architecture, and landscape design at UCLA, and president of Environmental Design Associates. ❧

Professor Koichi Kawana in 1981.

Five-foot Hida Snow Lantern.

1978

Denver Bonsai Club obtains a permit from the U.S. Forest Service to collect suitable character pines for the Japanese Garden. A delegation from Takayama, Japan, headed by Mayor Kichiro Mirata, presents the city and Gardens with a 5-foot-high, 1,760-pound Hida Snow Lantern, which is accepted by Mayor Bill McNichols. The Weckbaugh family donates funds for a Japanese tea house in memory of Mrs. Ella Mullen Weckbaugh, and Koichi Kawana personally orders the house in Japan. ❧

Japanese Garden Tea House, 1979 or 1980.

Construction begins on the Rock Alpine Garden, designed by Herb Schaal, consulting landscape architect from Eckbo, Dean, Austin, and Williams (EDAW) of San Francisco. ❧

Rock Alpine Garden.

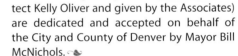
Margaret E. "Marnie" Honnen.

1981

In January, Marnie's Pavilion, at the west end of the conservatory, is dedicated as a memorial to board member Margaret E. "Marnie" Honnen. The pavilion was designed by Hornbein and White to house the Gardens' collection of bromeliads and orchids. ❧

In June, the Scripture Garden (designed by Jane Silverstein Ries, featuring Jewish and Christian artwork by William Joseph of Denver, and funded by the Coors Foundation), the Home Demonstration Garden (designed by Charles Randolph and given by the Garden Club of Denver) and the Rock Alpine Garden and Alpine House (the latter designed by architect Kelly Oliver and given by the Associates) are dedicated and accepted on behalf of the City and County of Denver by Mayor Bill McNichols. ❧

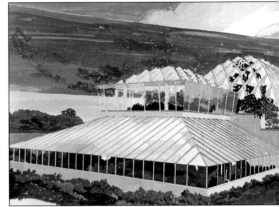
Architect's drawing of Marnie's Pavilion.

7

1979

On June 23, Shofu-en ("Garden of Pine and Wind"), the first authentic Japanese garden in the Rocky Mountain region, is dedicated. Master Soju Takahashi, sponsored by the Urasenke Foundation of Kyoto, officiates at the ritual tea ceremony in the Tea House. ❧

1980

In June, United Bank of Cherry Creek, radio station KCFR, and Denver Botanic Gardens launch a summer concert series of six chamber music concerts in the Gardens' amphitheatre. ❧

1983

In February, the Colorado Water Garden Society (the world's first water garden society) is founded at Denver Botanic Gardens. Thanks to plant donations by William Tricker, Inc. and Van Ness Water Gardens, the aquatic ornamental collection increases to more than 200 plants. ❧

Japanese Garden (Shofu-En) dedication.

Right: A typical summer concert.

8

Tiffany china.

1984

In September, benefit festivities, known as the Fête des Fleurs to honor the founding trustees, include a tea and a dinner dance. Table settings are provided by Tiffany & Co. ❧

Botanical author and illustrator Angela Overy begins to teach classes in botanical art and illustration. ❧

1986

Board President Edward P. Connors is instrumental in the introduction by Colorado Representative Pat Grant of House Bill 1138, "An Act concerning the Establishment of a Scientific and Cultural Facilities District." ❧

Edward P. Connors.

1988

In September, Chatfield Arboretum opens to the public on a limited basis with an open house that is attended by 650 people. ❧

In November, voters approve the creation of the Scientific and Cultural Facilities District, revenues from which will be received by the Gardens the following year. ❧

1985

Denver Botanic Gardens is awarded its first accreditation by the American Association of Museums, one of only ten gardens in the United States to obtain such accreditation. ❧

Larry Latta and the horticulture team string tiny white lights in the trees along the Linden-Allé, a precurser to Blossoms of Light. ❧

1987

Denver Botanic Gardens joins the Center for Plant Conservation. ❧

Through the Plant Evaluation and Introduction Program, test plants of three promising species are shipped to sixty-two cooperating nurseries for their evaluation and comments in preparation for introducing the plants to regional horticulturists. ❧

The Bonfils-Stanton Foundation underwrites a program of "nationally recognized speakers on botanical and horticultural topics of a popular nature." ❧

1989

The first Pumpkin Festival attracts 2,400 people to the newly renovated Deer Creek School at Chatfield Arboretum. ❧

"Blossoms of Light" during winter holidays.

Top: Annual Pumpkin Festival at the Gardens' Chatfield site. Above: Deer Creek Schoolhouse.

1990

The Certificate Program for Botanical Art and Illustration, one of just a handful nationwide, is established by Angela Overy and Rob Proctor.

1991

A new 25-year cooperative agreement between Denver Botanic Gardens and the City and County of Denver is signed, giving the Gardens' foundation control of its staffing, budgets, and programs.

1992

Construction begins on the Krohn office building north of the conservatory.

1995

The Birdhaus Bash, a birdhouse design and building competition attracts 320 people to the preview party and auction.

The Water-Smart Garden, funded by Denver Water and Metro Water Conservation, Inc., is dedicated.

Lauren Springer and Rob Proctor design the O'Fallon Perennial Border, a gift of the Martin J. and Mary Anne O'Fallon Trust.

Panayoti Kelaidis is appointed plant evaluation coordinator, responsible for the Plant Select® program, a joint venture with Colorado State University and the Green Industry.

Panayoti Kelaidis.

1998

In August, the Romantic Gardens, designed by Environmental Planning and Design "to energize the senses," is dedicated at the Fête des Fleurs gala. Immediately, there is great demand for the site as a wedding location.

9

The Romantic Gardens.

1993

Lauren Springer designs the Water-Smart Garden south of Boettcher Memorial Tropical Conservatory.

Water-Smart Garden at York Street.

1996

Boettcher Memorial Tropical Conservatory receives a 25-year award of the Colorado Chapter of the American Institute of Architects.

1997

Denver Botanic Gardens receives its second accreditation from the American Association of Museums, becoming one of only twelve botanic gardens in the United States to achieve this distinction.

Plant Select,® a program designed to seek out and distribute the very best plants from the High Plains to the intermountain region, launches its effort with five plant selections; more than 100,000 plants are produced and sold through regional garden centers.

O'Fallon Perennial Border, with Waring House in the distance.

A botanical illustration exhibit of more than 175 works is mounted to honor artist Anne Ophelia Dowden, who attends.

Anne Ophelia Dowden.

Boettcher Memorial Education Building as seen in 1973.

Drop-Dead Red Border.

1999
Tom Peace, hired by new horticulture director Rob Proctor, designs a Mile High Garden along York Street. Proctor himself designs a Drop-Dead Red Border along the north side of the pond next to Monet Garden.

2001
The Gardens celebrates its fiftieth anniversary and hosts the annual meeting of the American Association of Botanical Gardens and Arboreta and the Council on Botanical and Horticultural Libraries.

In March, a new expansion of the Boettcher Memorial Education Building and a new Gates Lecture Hall are completed.

The Gardens enters into a joint venture with Cherry Creek Shopping Center to provide interiorscaping.

Interiorscaping at Cherry Creek Shopping Center.

2003
In January, the Cloud Forest Tree in Marnie's Pavilion opens to showcase orchids and other epiphyte collections.

The misty Cloud Forest Tree.

2000
Mayor Wellington Webb asks the Gardens to partner with Denver Parks and Recreation to design Centennial Gardens, a 5-acre public garden located along the South Platte River at Speer Boulevard.

Three new gardens that celebrate native flora are implemented: Western Panoramas, Wildflower Treasures, and Sacred Earth. Other new gardens include: June's PlantAsia, Children's Secret Path, and the Cutting Garden.

Corn is planted on 5 acres of land at Denver Botanic Gardens at Chatfield to create the first Corn Maze, which runs for two months.

Above: Centennial Gardens, a French-inspired formal garden. Left: Corn maze with 2003 SCFD theme.

2002
During the driest years on record, the unirrigated Laura Smith Porter Plains Garden and Dryland Mesa feature abundant blooms and suffer no loss of plants.

A Gardens-wide plant inventory is initiated using a collection management database called BG-BASE.™

2003 (continued)
In April, June's PlantAsia is dedicated to former trustee June S. Gates. It features plants of Sino-Himalayan mountain flora, as well as from the dry semi-arid continental parts of Asia.

June's PlantAsia.

2003 (continued)

Research staff members establish two populations of the rare prairie gentian *(Eustoma grandiflorum)* in natural areas of the Rocky Mountain Arsenal. ❧

Prairie gentian (Edstoma grandiflorum).

2004

Scientific and Cultural Facilities District is reauthorized until 2016. ❧

In August, the Sensory Garden is dedicated as a public demonstration and teaching garden for horticultural therapy. ❧

Sensory Garden (Morrison Center).

2003 (continued)

The Dos Chappell Nature Center at Mount Goliath opens. ❧

Looking down on Dos Chappell Nature Center.

2005

In partnership with the United States Botanic Garden, Denver Botanic Gardens launches the Applied Plant Conservation Program to build collaborations across botanic gardens. ❧

Denver Botanic Gardens at Chatfield becomes an affiliate of the Lady Bird Johnson Wildflower Center. ❧

The Daniel and Janet Mordecai Foundation donates $1.3 million to provide the lead gift for supporting a new children's garden. ❧

At the request of Denver Mayor John Hickenlooper, the Gardens designs four water-smart gardens at the Denver City and County Building, and one each at Harvey Park Recreation Center, Highlands Senior Recreation Center, and Montbello Recreation Center. ❧

The All-America Selections Garden opens to display the best annual flower and vegetable varieties that have proven successful in the Colorado climate. ❧

2006

The Kathryn Kalmbach Herbarium's collection exceeds 43,000 species, and the Herbarium of Fungi, more than 22,000 species. A special reference collection of Colorado species is maintained to better help the public identify plants collected in the state. ❧

The High-Altitude Gardener website provides information on some 300 of the best plants for the Rocky Mountain region. ❧

2007

In September, the Carol Gossard Colorado Native Plant Garden is dedicated at Chatfield.

Donor and dedicated Gardens supporter, Carol Gossard.

The Board of Directors unanimously approves a 25-year Master Development Plan.

In November, voters approve a "Better Denver" bond initiative that provides $18.6 million to Denver Botanic Gardens to refurbish the irrigation system, build new greenhouses, and improve public safety and accessibility.

Plant Select® sells more than 1.5 million plants in North America, and transitions to a new organizational structure as a nonprofit corporation.

Supporters of bond initiative in 2007.

2008

Four core values of a new branding platform—transformation, relevance, diversity, and sustainability—spell out the Gardens' intentions for the years ahead.

The $42.9 million Flourish Capital Campaign to fund the Master Development Plan is launched with a $1.5 million gift from the Bonfils-Stanton Foundation. In appreciation, the Gardens names the planned visitor center the Bonfils-Stanton Visitor Center.

Denver Botanic Gardens is re-accredited by the American Association of Museums and commended: "The Garden is a model organization." (James A. Welu, Chair, Accreditation Commission, AAM)

2007 (continued)

In April, Brian Vogt is hired as chief executive officer.

The horticulture staff creates a green roof over the Gift Shop.

Brian Vogt, hired as CEO in 2007.

Green roof demonstrates environmental sustainability.

Sources

Archives of Denver Botanic Gardens.

Denver Botanic Gardens, *Annual Reports* (1973–2007).

Denver Botanic Gardens Long Range Planning Committee, *Long Range Framework Plan,* Volume 1. June 16, 2004, pp. B-2 through B-11.

Denver Botanic Gardens website, http://www.botanicgardens.org/content/history

The Green Thumb, vol. 1 (1944) through vol. 46 (1989).

The Green Thumb Newsletter (1974–1997).

Morley, Judy, *Oasis in the City: The History of Denver Botanic Gardens.* Thesis submitted to the faculty of the graduate school of the University of Colorado at Denver, in partial fulfillment of the requirements for the degree of Master of Arts History, 1995.

Peterson, Bernice E., "A Jubilee History of Denver Botanic Gardens," in *Cemetery to Conservatory: A History of Land Around Denver Botanic Gardens 1859–1978,* by Louisa Ward Arps. (Denver, CO: Denver Botanic Gardens, 1980).

Early Visionaries

Overview by *Panayoti Kelaidis* · Biographies by *Deb Golanty*

FIFTY YEARS AGO, when Dr. A. C. Hildreth penned the words used in the dedication of this book, he was the only paid staff member of Denver Botanic Gardens. Today, well over one hundred staff keep the organization humming year around (far more, of course, in the busy summer season), and over a thousand volunteers join them as the engine that drives the Gardens. Plants are the focus and raison d'être of a botanic garden, but people are the ones who must champion the plants and who marshal the forces to study, steward, and enjoy these plants. Many people laid the groundwork for the creation of Denver Botanic Gardens at York Street more than fifty years ago. We have selected four giants —early visionaries—who might be said to have set in motion and pointed the direction in which we are still headed today.

Ruth Porter Waring donated the mansion that bears her family name, which served as the headquarters, library, offices—everything—until the conservatory and education buildings were completed almost a decade later. Her history and connections, as well as those of a number of other women, especially Katherine B. Crisp (Mrs. William H. Crisp), Gladys C. Evans (Mrs. John Evans), Helen Fowler (Mrs. John Fowler), and Anna R. Garrey (Mrs. George H. Garrey)—many of them members of the Garden Club of America—were essential in the politically delicate task of transforming a pioneer cemetery into a botanic garden.

It would be hard to imagine the Gardens' creation without a half-century of constant campaigning by two landscape architects born in the Netherlands. *The Green Thumb News*, a bulletin published by the Colorado Forestry and Horticulture Association, which eventually incorporated as the Botanical Gardens Foundation of Denver, is peppered with articles written by M. Walter Pesman and Saco DeBoer, explaining the rationale of a botanic garden, arguing for its creation and laying down a blueprint, as it were, of our future. Both of these inspired individuals contributed to Denver's efforts in a burgeoning nationwide City Beautiful movement—a municipal reform to establish coordinated beautification and planning programs. Pesman's passion for native plants and naturalistic design imbues much of what we do today. DeBoer designed and oversaw the creation and planting of the Gates Montane Garden, the first garden at York Street. His enormous vision of a city in harmony with the mountains and plains provides the underpinnings not only of Denver Botanic Gardens, but the hundreds of miles of parkways and parks that he designed and planted at the behest of Mayor Speer. He can truly be said to be the father of horticulture in Colorado.

George Kelly was the first acting director of Denver Botanic Gardens when it came into being, and his feisty, almost bellicose personality at times seems to linger in the walls and echo through the pathways of this institution. His endless enthusiasm for connecting plants and people, especially of the Rocky Mountain region, literally morphed into our mission statement. "Rocky Mountain Horticulture is Different" was not only the title of his book, the bible of many generations of local gardeners, but the principle that informs and distinguishes our Gardens from those anywhere else in America or beyond. It is perhaps no accident that an institution created by personalities like these still flourishes. ❧

George W. Kelly

Born on May 8, 1894, in Scotch Ridge, Ohio, George Whitfield Kelly was one of six sons of a wayward evangelist. While it was horticulture, not religion, that fueled Kelly's highly articulate, lifelong drive to inspire an audience, it is safe to assume that Kelly came by his zeal naturally.

"I have been preaching the idea that 'Rocky Mountain horticulture is different' for some forty years now," he once said while lecturing at Denver Botanic Gardens. "A few people are beginning to get the idea and find that they can have as good gardens and parks here as any place in the world, if they learn to design their gardens, select the plants to construct them, and learn how these plants, in a way, fit Colorado's distinctive climate." For his enduring work and vision, Kelly is known as "the man who taught us how to garden."

Kelly came to Colorado by way of Salinas, Kansas, where he worked as a baggage clerk on the Union Pacific Railroad. In April 1919, he started a new job potting plants in the greenhouses at Elitch Gardens in Denver. After several stints around the state, he went to work back in Denver at the Denver Wholesale Florists and later at the Rocky Mountain Seed Company. He continued studying landscaping and drafting by mail. In 1927, he was hired by Denver Public Schools as a landscape gardener, and there he met M. Walter Pesman. Through Pesman's work with the Colorado State Highway Department, Kelly became involved with roadside parks and highway beautification.

The Pesman's funded Kelly in a nursery business venture called Arapahoe Acres, which, from an inauspicious beginning in 1932, became a prosperous business through 1944. Kelly's customers enjoyed $100 worth of plant knowledge with each sale of even a 50-cent plant. During this period, Kelly found his voice, speaking to gardening clubs and doing a talk show on KOA radio called Green Thumb. His writing career took off with a series of gardening articles in the *Littleton Independent*.

When the Colorado Forestry and Horticulture Association (CFHA) was created from the merger of the Colorado Forestry Association and the Denver Society of Ornamental Horticulture, Kelly was one of its founders, as well as its first full-time horticulturist. According to biographer Wes Woodward, "All of George Kelly's love of the West and its plants, his unflagging energy, his urge to develop and improve all that he touched, was concentrated into the intense devotion and effort he gave the association in the next twelve years." As the first editor of *The Green Thumb News*, George wrote for that magazine and developed it into an authoritative publication. During his editorship from 1944 to 1955, he authored eighty-two major articles in that publication. His theme—to preach the gospel of adjusting gardening in Colorado to the state's unusual conditions.

"I worked there eleven years, trying two kinds of education: to educate the people who *claim* to know something about horticulture—the nurserymen and landscapers—to really know something about it, and to educate the people to appreciate the difference about the people who knew something about it and those who didn't," he reflected in a 1981 interview. "*Nobody knew the difference!* The horticultural ignorance in Denver was shocking."

Urged by his friends, Kelly put his talks and writings into book form, whose publication was funded by Helen Fowler, Mrs. Churchill Owen, and Don Peach. In 1951 the book *Rocky Mountain Horticulture is Different* was published. The book quickly gained a reputation as "the bible" on regional plants and gardening. Observed Kelly, "People think our sunshine, cool nights, unpredictable springs and falls, open winters, and dry air are ideal. People can listen to the weatherman and decide what to wear. Plants aren't so lucky. So we have to modify the effects of the sun, wind, heat, and cold." At $1 a copy, it sold out quickly. Kelly followed with several other successful books on similar themes, most notably *Good Gardens for the Sunshine States* (1957) and *Rocky Mountain Horticulture* (1992).

With others in the CFHA, Kelly worked toward the establishment of a botanic garden. When CFHA merged into Denver Botanic Gardens, Kelly, then a charter trustee, was hired as its first acting director. In 1951, Sue Johnson, a widow working on the herbarium committee, became Kelly's secretary at Horticulture House. She was an accomplished horticulturist in her own right, and on May 16, 1952, the two married.

Finding institutional duties constraining, in 1955 Kelly returned to the nursery business. He owned and successfully operated the Cottonwood Garden Shop in Littleton. Subsequently, in 1965 he and his wife moved to McElmo Canyon in Cortez, Colorado. There, on 100 acres, they gardened, farmed, and in 1967, contributed a master plan for the beautification of Cortez.

Kelly loved Colorado and keenly understood the challenges and vulnerability of the region. He was especially prescient on the subject of water conservation. "Our emphasis is very much [on] water," he observed in 1981, "because we know that sooner or later people are going to have to get along with less water per each because there is not more water available in the state. As we get a greater population we're going to have to divide that water up among a greater number of people."

At the end of his passionate, productive life, Kelly enjoyed a shower of professional accolades. In 1986, when he was ninety-two, nearly two-thousand members of the American Association of Nurserymen honored him with the Jane Silverstein Ries award for "his dedicated service as educator, writer, adviser, and friend to the nursery industry." In 1990, Ft. Lewis College in Durango awarded him its first-ever honorary degree in Southwestern Horticulture. Kelly died on August 10, 1991, at the age of ninety-seven.

Michiel Walter Pesman

"He made the native plants our friends." So reads the memorial plaque honoring Michiel Walter Pesman on the trail named for him on Mount Goliath—a man distinguished by his passion for life, artistry in his profession as landscape architect, his prodigious outpouring of articles and books, his teaching, as well as his tireless commitment to horticulture, conservation and Denver Botanic Gardens.

Michiel Walter Pesman was born in Thesinge, Groningen, The Netherlands, on May 28, 1887. His higher education was halted for a year by tuberculosis, and when he recovered, he emigrated to the United States. In 1908 he was admitted to the Colorado Agricultural College, from which he graduated in 1910 with a major in botany.

His first name was difficult for Americans to pronounce correctly, so Pesman became a naturalized citizen under the name M. Walter Pesman. He began his professional career as a landscape architect with the Chamberlain Landscaping Co. in Denver. By 1917, he was secretary of the Denver Society for Ornamental Horticulture, writing for its publication, *Garden Hints*, as well as for the Colorado Forestry Association. His interests were varied as illustrated by the articles he penned: "A Landscape Architect's Views on Highway Planting," "Stopping Tree Waste—Facts and Needs," "Trees of Boulder, Colorado," and "Almost Anything Can Be Made of Wood."

In 1919, Pesman opened an office in Denver's Tramway building with fellow Dutchman Saco Rienk DeBoer, a collaboration of landscape architects that, according to George Kelly, "was remarkable that this partnership continued as long as it did because their philosophies were so different." A year after Pesman's marriage in 1923 to Anna Elizabeth Hyde, a Denver school teacher, the firm dissolved. Said DeBoer, "We had a hard time pioneering landscape architecture in a pioneer city. We had work but very little money." Pesman took over the firm's contract with Denver schools, and, "with sparkling enthusiasm and rare energy," planned the grounds for these buildings: Byers Junior High School, Ebert, Bryant-Webster, South High and East High.

When the Depression slowed landscape work for Denver schools, Pesman applied his planning talents to joint projects of the State Highway Department and the Federal government. His work ranged from revegetation of eroding highway slopes to the creation of roadside parks. According to his new collaborator, George Kelly, who worked with Pesman for close to 40 years, "At first [Pesman] had difficulties in getting plans approved in Washington that had native plants in them, for they were unknown back there. Later, when the survival lists were checked, nothing but natives would be approved."

In addition to highway work, Pesman designed the Memorial Park at Crown Hill Cemetery; Country Club Gardens on Downing Street; many city and zoning plans; as well as designs for private homes. He taught classes in landscape architecture, botany and horticulture at the University of Denver and Colorado State University. "There was never a time when he wasn't teaching somewhere, at least once a week, often more than that. He was well educated, had a great vocabulary, loved people. The young people who came to hear him loved him," said Orland Maxson, a draftsman-artist who worked for him.

Regardless of his other commitments, Pesman and his wife never stopped investigating native plants of the Rockies. His meticulously documented collection of specimens was illustrated by Maxson, leading to the publication of *Meet the Natives* in 1942. This friendly work of text and drawings was intended to aid the user in properly identifying more than 400 native plants growing in the Rocky Mountains. Said Pesman modestly in his introduction: "Just between you and me—don't buy this book if you know too much. It is not a book for botanists." Nonetheless, the book was not only an immediate success but was revised and updated through ten editions. (An eleventh edition is now in preparation by Denver Botanic Gardens.)

In 1943, Pesman was president of the Colorado Forestry Association and brought about the consolidation of forestry, horticulture, gardening and landscaping interests to form the Colorado Forestry and Horticulture Association, serving as its first president. As a member of its Board of Directors, he was instrumental in the merging of the organization with Denver Botanic Gardens Inc., on whose Board of Trustees he actively served. He also wrote 110 articles that were published in *The Green Thumb News*, between the years 1944 and 1968. In 1961, the Board voted him an honorarium for his services, but he refused "to be singled out in an achievement to which so many members of the editorial committee contributed … I must live my life on principles I have outlined for myself … and which I have tried to follow."

Coming full circle, in April 1958, Pesman addressed the Fifteenth International Horticultural Congress in Nice, France, on his favorite subject, the flora of the Rocky Mountain region. He identified the plants growing in this "intemperate, arid, alkaline region" and proposed that many could be grown in Europe. "It is," he said, "an almost unexplored field of plant introductions." He then distributed packets of columbine seed. In 1959, he was elected a Fellow of the Royal Horticultural Society of London.

Pesman lived to see the publication of his second book, *Meet Flora Mexicana*, before his death in November 1962. To his family and friends, he wrote: "All the past is prologue; the glorious future is still ahead, and you, I am sure, are doing your share in making it truly worth while for all. Good luck to all of you, my very dear friends and relatives!"

Ruth Porter Waring

"Gardening is *creative*—just as painting a picture is creative." These words, spoken by Ruth Porter Waring in a 1969 interview on behalf of Denver Botanic Gardens, sum up her vision for the institution she loved so well. "We have a big job to teach citizens of Denver we're not just another big garden," she said. "We're an organization for education and research work."

Ruth Porter Waring was born in Denver in 1889, and attended the Miss Wolcott School in Denver and Mount Vernon Seminary in Washington, D.C. Her father, Henry Miller Porter, was a successful entrepreneur who retired at the age of seventy-nine. He divided his assets equally among his five children and devoted the rest of his life to worthy causes. Biographer Patricia Paton notes that "[Porter's] philanthropies were fired by his belief, shared with Andrew Carnegie, that the man who dies rich dies disgraced." His example might well have inspired his daughter Ruth's lifelong civic passion.

On June 15, 1921, Ruth Porter married Dr. James Johnston Waring. The prior February, a *Rocky Mountain News* society column had noted:

> Society will be particularly interested in the betrothal of Miss Ruth Porter. Miss Porter, who occupies a prominent position in exclusive Denver society, is sojourning in La Jolla, California, with her parents at present. She is unusually charming and clever and takes an active part in the social life of Denver.

Throughout her long life, Ruth Porter Waring was extraordinarily involved in the social and, most especially, the civic life of Denver. "Once her interest is aroused in a cause she will bend every effort to make it a success," said a 1941 *Rocky Mountain News* article, "But very quietly, for she shuns personal publicity."

She helped establish the Children's Hospital in 1912, was active in the American Red Cross during World War I, and financially supported both the Webb-Waring Lung Institute and Porter Hospital (founded by her father). In 1927, she co-founded Denver's Graland Country Day School. She was a principal benefactor of the Central City Opera Association and a life trustee of the Denver Symphony Orchestra.

Her greatest efforts, however, were devoted to Denver Botanic Gardens, to which she gave generously of her time, energy, and money for more than a quarter century. She was a charter trustee, participating in the arrangements between the Botanical Gardens Foundation and the City of Denver, which led to establishing a botanical garden on the old Calvary Cemetery grounds in 1951. In 1958, the Warings purchased the house at 909 York Street and donated it the following year as an administrative building for the Gardens.

In 1971, at the age of eighty-two, Mrs. Waring contributed her husband's collection of rare botanical books along with the funds to provide a room for them in the Helen Fowler Library of the Gardens' Education Building. Today, the Waring Rare Book Room contains Dr. Waring's original collection plus additional books and archival materials important to the Gardens' history.

The Gardens' Boettcher Memorial Tropical Conservatory, auxiliary greenhouses, and laboratories were possible in part because of Mrs. Waring's contributions. In addition, she supported the children's gardening program and the Plains Garden, given in memory of her mother, Laura Smith Porter.

Other organizations that benefited from her membership and efforts include the Garden Club of Denver, Denver Orchid Society, Ikebana International, and Denver Rose Society. Her interest in plants and her organizational skills and concern for detail are obvious from the botany class notes, hundreds of file cards on plant characteristics, planting plans for her own gardens, and the many slides of plants that are among her papers in the Rare Book Room.

On her one-hundredth birthday, the Gardens' Board of Trustees honored her by putting her name on the shrub *Prunus tenella* 'Ruth's 100th'—a plant "as hardy and resistant to the vicissitudes of the Colorado climate as is our dearly beloved Ruth Porter Waring to the vicissitudes of time." An iris—*Iris* 'Mrs. Ruth Porter Waring'—was named after her in 1986. And each year, she is remembered by employees of Denver Botanic Gardens attending the annual Mrs. Waring's Holiday Party, which she endowed, an event featuring "Mrs. Waring's punch."

Ruth Porter Waring died on December 27, 1992. She was 103.

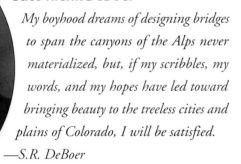

Saco Rienk DeBoer

My boyhood dreams of designing bridges to span the canyons of the Alps never materialized, but, if my scribbles, my words, and my hopes have led toward bringing beauty to the treeless cities and plains of Colorado, I will be satisfied.
—*S.R. DeBoer*

The city of Denver, Colorado, will likely never know another landscape architect and planner more prolific than Saco Rienk (S.R.) DeBoer. His career spanned the fruitful administrations of mayors Speer and Stapleton in Denver, expanded to other cities and states in the West, and encompassed both public and private projects that are his enduring legacy.

Born on September 7, 1883, in the Dutch city of Ureterp, DeBoer studied landscape architecture at The Royal Imperial School of Horticulture in Germany. In 1907, he started his own landscaping firm, but the next year he contracted tuberculosis. Advised by his doctors to seek a healthy climate in the United States, he traveled to Maxwell City, New Mexico, and shortly thereafter to Denver, where he thrived until he was almost ninety-one. He was known to say that he never spent a day ill in America.

When DeBoer became Denver's consultant landscape architect and city planner in 1910, the city's 213,000 people enjoyed 1,100 acres of parks, most of which were open pasture. When he resigned his post in 1957, Denver's 500,000 people took pleasure in about 2,500 acres of beautifully improved park systems, as well as landscaped corridors such as Monaco Parkway, East Seventeenth Avenue, and Speer Boulevard. In those forty-seven years, he influenced, planned, and supervised the development of Denver's famous park and parkway systems, most notably under the administration of Mayor Speer.

DeBoer made the case for beautiful landscape architecture in very practical terms. "Develop parks and parkways," he told Mayor Speer in 1910, "and you will make Denver a place people will want to visit."

During Mayor Speer's terms as mayor (from 1910 to 1918), DeBoer planted what can be thought of as signature trees along many city streets and developed the initial landscape plans for Washington Park; Cheesman Park; the grounds of the state capitol building and nearby civic center; and Denver Botanical Gardens at City Park, to name a few. Following the death of Mayor Speer in 1918, DeBoer went into partnership with M. Walter Pesman for five years, thereafter setting up his own private practice. In 1920, the City of Denver Parks and Recreation Department hired De-Boer as a consultant, a position he filled for more than three-and-a-half decades.

When Mayor Stapleton began his term as mayor in 1923, DeBoer continued his development of city parks. He directed the plantings of cottonwood trees, hedges, and flowerbeds along Speer Boulevard. He designed Alamo Placita Park at Ogden Street and Arlington Park (now called Hungarian Freedom Park).

In 1949, DeBoer prepared *A Master Plan for Denver's Parks*, a work that captured his vision for five park districts and proposed a long-range program for future development. Of note is his idea that "attention must be paid to establishing long trails through the parks, from one park to another, and from the city to the mountains." His confidence in his plan is evident in the statement that "the program outlined here should suffice Denver's development for fifty years; in other words, to the year 2000."

Through the years, DeBoer maintained an active private practice, doing many residential as well as civic designs. In the latter capacity, he served as a consultant planner for the state of Wyoming, the U.S. Department of Agriculture, and the National Park Service, as well as the National Resources Planning Board for New Mexico, Wyoming, and Utah. He worked as a city planner in many growing towns and cities throughout the West.

DeBoer had made an eloquent case for city planning in a small but extraordinary book published in 1937 called *Shopping Districts*. "As a civilization we face the peculiar fact that we are able to design skyscrapers of unlimited height … but that in the design of one single block of business houses we cannot, as yet, produce anything that is either attractive or even practical," he wrote, arguing for logical integration and appropriate scale in the design of commercial city centers. He advocated such concepts as "natural zoning," "the business district as a place for social gathering" and planning with respect to "the very heart of the city." Anticipating the successful development of such inner city districts as Denver's Larimer Square, he noted, "In some cities quaint little streets of historical value have been used successfully for the location of unique restaurants."

He envisioned that Denver be made beautiful by planning and greenery, critical to which was a botanical garden:

No large city should be without a botanical garden. It becomes the experimental station for trees, flowering plants, and everything that grows in the region. It has immense educational value and may influence the commercial growing of flowers and trees, of fruit, vegetables, and farm crops to such an extent as to give the regions new sources of livelihood. … A botanical garden, carefully designed, holds as much landscape interest as a park and can give service as a park as well as a botanical collection.

DeBoer chaired the Botanic Garden Committee of the Colorado Forestry Association, which resolved in 1941 to form a botanic garden. In 1951, he was hired by Mr. and Mrs. John Evans to design the fifteen-year, $1.5 million master plan that was accepted by city council to be built on 100 acres in the southeast corner of City Park. DeBoer's plan featured a canyon, alpines, and, among other large plant collections, no fewer than forty-seven flowering crabapples.

DeBoer had a passion for plants, which he captured in a modest but influential book called *Around the Seasons in Denver Parks and Gardens*, published in 1948. "For many years it has been my dream to write the story of the unfolding seasons in Denver and surroundings," he says. "I have tried to describe the things to look for at each period [i.e., season] and places to find them. … Do not judge it too severely; it is neither a scientific book nor a novel, neither a textbook nor a handbook, it is just a little book for your enjoyment, just as I have enjoyed writing it."

DeBoer received many awards, but perhaps the one that best captures his achievements was the 1960 Distinguished Service Award of the American Institute of Planners. It lauded his "contribution to the literature of planning, including pioneer studies of downtown revitalization and the improvement of metropolitan and regional planning policies." DeBoer, renowned as "the man who beautified Denver," remained active in city planning, landscape architecture, and planting until his death on August 16, 1974.

Sources

George W. Kelly

Denver Post, February 8, 1972, p. 12

—. July 22, 1986, p. 1B

—. August 14, 1991, p. 7B.

"George W. Kelly: A Year of Awards." *The Green Thumb News* 41:1:1987 (Spring/Summer), p. 13

"Interview with George Kelly." *Colorado Green* (Fall 1981), pp. 9–30.

Krieger, George W., "Four brown fingers and a green thumb." *The Denver Westerners Roundup* (January-February 1992), pp. 3–18.

"Local Botanists Honored." *The Green Thumb News* 36:4:1979 (Winter), p. 124.

Woodward, Wes, "The man who taught us how to garden." *The Green Thumb News* 31:2: 1974 (Summer), pp. 42–47.

Michiel Walter Pesman

Denver Post, November 18, 1962, p. 35C.

"In Memoriam—M. Walter Pesman" and "In Retrospect." *The Green Thumb News* 20:1:1963 (Jan.-Feb.), pp. 6–8

"M. Walter Pesman, F.R.H.S." *The Green Thumb News* 16:6:1959 (July), p. 195.

"The M. Walter Pesman Nature Trail." *The Green Thumb News* 21:6:1964 (August-September), p. 201.

Woodward, Wes, "M. Walter Pesman: He Made the Native Plants Our Friends." *The Green Thumb News* 32:3:1975 (Autumn), pp. 75–83.

Ruth Porter Waring

"A Resolution in honor of Mrs. Ruth Porter Waring." *The Green Thumb News* 33:1:15 (Spring 1976).

Denver Post, December 15, 1969, p. 25

Excerpts from "Ruth Porter Waring: A Closer Look at a Beloved Benefactor of the Gardens," Mary Lou Waldman, *Inside the Gardens*, January/February 2007, p. 12.

Paton, Patricia. *A Medical Gentleman: James J. Waring M.D.* (Denver, CO: Colorado Historical Society, 1993); see page 64 for quote.

Rocky Mountain News, March 16, 1941, p. 7.

Saco Rienk DeBoer

Falkenberg, Janis, "De Boer Remembered." *The Green Thumb News* 40:3:1983 (Autumn), pp. 217–222.

"Plants, Parks and People—S.R. DeBoer." *The Green Thumb News* 29:5:1972 (December), pp. 142–225.

"S.R. DeBoer Park." *The Green Thumb News* 19:6:1962 (July), p. 204.

Summers, Joyce, "One Man's Vision: Saco Rienk DeBoer, Denver Landscape Architect." *Colorado Heritage* (1988), pp. 28–42; see page 40 for quote about botanical garden.

Woodward, Wes, "S.R. DeBoer (1883–1974), *The Green Thumb News* 31:4: 1974 (Winter), p. 132.

Plant Portraits

The plants that one encounters in gardens and nurseries
in the Front Range area of Colorado, and elsewhere in our region,
are utterly different from what one would have encountered fifty years ago.
A large proportion of the native and adapted plants utilized nowadays
in American gardens debuted on the grounds of Denver Botanic Gardens.
Many of these plants simply are not found in common reference books
or even on the Internet. We present here an assortment of plants
introduced over the history of Denver Botanic Gardens with ways
to use them in the garden. Each plant description is accompanied
by beautiful color photographs and hand-painted renderings
from the gifted artists from DBG's Botanical art program.

All photos, unless otherwise indicated,
were taken by the Gardens' official photographer,
Scott Dressel-Martin.

Alpine Columbine

Aquilegia saximontana Rydb.
Ranunculaceae

By *Mike Kintgen*, Horticulturist, Denver Botanic Gardens

Picture a more delicate miniature than the Colorado columbine and you have *Aquilegia saximontana*. Native only to the state of Colorado in rock fields at higher elevations, this exquisite little columbine happens to be the emblem of the Rocky Mountain Chapter of the North American Rock Garden Society. Despite its delicate demeanor, this columbine has proven to be an adaptable addition to gardens at both high and low elevations throughout the West, and works well in rock gardens, troughs, and along paths.

Pendant blue and white dove-like blooms gently nod on a plant with finely cut leaves. It blooms in early May to mid-June at lower elevations, and in late June through August in its native habitat. Occasionally a few blooms reappear in the fall at lower elevations.

While it is not clear exactly when *Aquilegia saximontana* entered general cultivation, it is known that after it was accepted as the emblem of the local rock garden society it became a regular at local nurseries and plant sales. Columbine are not particularly long lived at lower elevations, generally averaging two to five years. If you have the right spot you may have seedlings that carry on; however, if you grow other columbine you could end up with some interesting hybrids involving *A. saximontana* and those others.

HEIGHT	5–15 inches (usually at the lower end of this spectrum)
WIDTH	5–12 inches
BLOOMS	May to August
SUN	Part shade to full sun (if shaded by a rock from noon day sun)
SOIL MOISTURE	Moderate
HARDINESS	USDA zone 1 (extreme heat is more of a problem; not a plant for hot, humid cities) (to 12,000 feet or more)
CULTURE	Clay-loam to sandy; will not tolerate standing water around the crown

Location at the Gardens: Denver Botanic Gardens has grown *Aquilegia saximontana* since at least 1979 in a variety of locations. Currently the best gardens to see it are Wildflower Treasures and the north slope of the Cactus and Succulent House in the Rock Alpine Garden.

25

Pine-mat Manzanita

Arctostaphylos nevadensis A. Gray
Ericaceae

By *Michael Bone*, Senior Horticulturist, Greenhouse and Propagation, Denver Botanic Gardens

In California there are dozens of species and naturally occurring hybrids of manzanita. Few people were aware that Colorado had its own examples of these elegant broadleaf evergreens until they began to be displayed throughout Denver Botanic Gardens in the early 1980s. The oldest accessions are dated January 1979, when plants were acquired from the Vancouver Alpine Society. That original planting has since been relocated to allow for an extension of the South African Plaza, and again for the expansion of the dwarf and unusual conifer collection.

The taxonomy of this genus has been an interesting evolution over the last couple of years. There has been much debate as to what these plants really are, and how the distribution has taken place. What was once grown as *A. nevadensis* is now understood to be a naturally occurring hybrid known as *A.* x *coloradoensis*, and is extremely variable in nature. This unique variability has given rise to many of the wonderful selections now available from Plant Select.® Much of the early work on these plants was done by Denver Botanic Gardens' propagators and trialed in our Rock Alpine Garden and in the native gardens.

The true *A. nevadensis* is much more of a ground cover and has a very distinct morphology. Plants are rarely over 8 inches in height and can be found naturally cascading over rocks in the dappled under-story of pine forests. It is a feat for these plants to be able to come from the dry high elevations of California to be

HEIGHT	10–15 inches
WIDTH	36–60 inches
BLOOMS	February to April
SUN	Full sun to partial shade
SOIL MOISTURE	Xeric once established
HARDINESS	USDA zones 4b–8 (up to 7,000 feet)
CULTURE	Well-drained garden loam or sandy soil

utilized in our gardens here. Since there are so many manzanitas in the same range as the pine-mat, there are some beautiful hybrids, many of which will alter the bark coloration, leaf size, flowering time, and intensity. One of the best uses for *A. nevadensis* in the garden is spilling over a rock wall in a dry shady area where few other plants will grow because of the pine straw fallen from the trees above it.

Location at the Gardens: Grown mainly in the Rock Alpine Garden, but specimens can also be seen in the Dryland Mesa. There are also plantings in Shady Lane and the Gates Montane Garden.

Greenleaf Manzanita

Arctostaphylos patula Greene
Ericaceae

By *Michael Bone,* Senior Horticulturist, Greenhouse and Propagation, Denver Botanic Gardens

Our earliest accession for *A. patula* dates to 1980, acquired from western Colorado by Panayoti Kelaidis. *A. patula* has for a long time been one of the most sought after native broad-leaved evergreens. Pro-

duction difficulties make this one rare to find in local nurseries. There is, however, a great deal of potential for making some remarkable selections for plant size and flower color.

A. patula is the epitome of winter interest for the garden, blooming in late winter to early spring. It is often graced with colorful red berries in late summer and fall. The native range for this plant is throughout the West, from Montana to Arizona. In Colorado it is found growing on the Western Slope in hot and dry areas above 8,000 feet. I have seen some incredible populations on the Uncompaghre Plateau and in the Manti–La Sal National Forests around Buckeye Reservoir. Most of the Colorado forms of *A. patula* are in the 4 by 4-foot size range, and have flower colors ranging from white with soft blush tips to deep candy-apple red.

One of the attributes of this plant that I extol the most is the bark color and texture. Stems are almost the color of a true red-headed Irish girl's hair, and they are waxy to the point of looking wet. These plants make a very stately addition to

HEIGHT	24–56 inches
WIDTH	40–80 inches
BLOOMS	February to April
SUN	Full sun to partial shade
SOIL MOISTURE	Xeric once established
HARDINESS	USDA zones 4b–8 (up to 7,000 feet)
CULTURE	Well-drained garden loam or sandy soil

the native xeriscape, but do need a little protection from the desiccating winter winds that are so common along the Front Range. When you grow this plant in your own garden, either plant it on an east-facing slope or in dry shade. The European heathers all quiver enviously in the face of the American West's *Arctostaphylos'* unmistakable brilliance.

Location at the Gardens: Plants are grown on the east side of Dryland Mesa.

Blackberry Lily

Belamcanda chinensis (L.) DC.
Iridaceae

By *Matthew Cole,* Director of Education and Interpretation, Denver Botanic Gardens

It is easy enough to report that the blackberry lily first arrived at Denver Botanic Gardens as seed from Longwood Gardens in Pennsylvania. But those words capture nothing of any true encounter with the plant.

The seed pod is the obvious source of the common name "blackberry," as its dry, pear-shaped seed pods split apart to reveal shiny, round, black seeds in a tight cluster. Touch the seeds, and you immediately discover the exterior is not a succulent fruit but a dry, papery surface enclosing a hard seed.

The plant originated in Asia, so it's not native to the United States, but it is widely cultivated in the East. Truthfully, the plant is neither blackberry nor lily. The flower is six-petaled, like a lily, but *Belamcanda's* sword-like leaves reveal it as one of the Iris family instead. Imagine 10-inch *Gladiolus* leaves in flattened iris-like fans that are crowned by blooms of an entirely unexpected nature.

HEIGHT	30–48 inches
WIDTH	10–15 inches
BLOOMS	July to August
SUN	Full sun to partial shade
SOIL MOISTURE	Moderate
HARDINESS	USDA zones 4b–8 (up to 7,000 feet)
CULTURE	Well-drained garden loam or sandy soil

All the surprises don't matter if it will grow for you, and it does well in a wide variety of sunny garden environments, preferring moist, well-drained soil. Expect it to reach 3 or 4 feet from its rhizomes to the tip of its midsummer inflorescences. It's widely reported to be hardy through zone 5, but I've heard scattered reports of gardeners in colder climates sheltering renegades through a few years. The effort is undoubtedly worth it as soon as the buds open for them.

Compared to many garden lilies, the petals are of a smaller and more restrained shape. But the colors ... the colors rival all but the hottest of hot color combinations: yellow and orange bases war underneath a vigorous freckling of red-orange dots. They are colors that captivate the eye, invigorate the landscape, and energize a garden with a burst of interest. I've seen it capture visitors from a full stride to stock still in the blink of an eye. The word I've heard the blackberry lily most commonly inspire is "fun."

Is it any wonder that the plant has been at York Street continuously since 1977? Both seeds and cuttings have been received repeatedly over the years, but some plants even remain from the first lineage that arrived over thirty years ago.

Location at the Gardens: Plants can be found in the O'Fallon Perennial Border, Shady Lane, and June's PlantAsia.

American Hornbeam

Carpinus caroliniana Walter
Betulaceae

ILLUSTRATION BY: Katherine McCrery

By: *Michael Bone,* Senior Horticulturist, Greenhouse and Propagation, Denver Botanic Gardens

The American hornbeam is a common woodland species in the eastern portions of North America. There are two distinct subspecies that occur: *C. caroliniana* ssp. *caroliniana* and *C. caroliniana* ssp. *virginiana,* the former being found mostly in the southern states, while the latter is found north of the Mason-Dixon Line. The plants growing in the Waring House courtyard are from the Schichtels Nursery in New York, and were planted in June, 1983. Woody plants that extend such a wide native range will most always require very different conditions depending on provenance. Our accessions coming from New York have a much greater potential for cold tolerance than plants that might come from the interior of Florida.

This is another of those trees that could easily be planted purely for the interesting bark coloration and texture, even though the flowers and the fall color are nothing to scoff at. The trunks of *C. caroliniana* look like concrete replicas of real trees; they even feel like concrete. I often hear people complain about how unnatural cement is and how artificial it looks when they see buildings made from it, or how cold and impersonal it makes them feel. When I hear these statements I will often reflect on the American hornbeam and its shocking beauty—the clean lines and the graceful contrast of the soft green foliage and the stark gray of the bark. On occasion, I even give people short tours of two or three of my favorite trees

HEIGHT	10–20 feet
WIDTH	8–15 feet
BLOOMS	May (decorative fruit persist all growing season)
SUN	Full sun to partial shade
SOIL MOISTURE	Moderate
HARDINESS	USDA zones 4b–9 (up to 7,000 feet) depending on source
CULTURE	Well-drained garden loam or sandy soil

and show them how that natural concrete color is something to be desired and sought after.

The chartreuse pendulous catkins that form in the summer dance happily on the tips of the branches. *C. caroliniana* can be tricky to over-winter as a young plant, but given care and insulation on the coldest of nights in the juvenile stage, these plants will grow up to make conversation pieces in the garden. Perfectly suited for the protected courtyard, American hornbeams are favorites of squirrels and tree collectors alike.

Location at the Gardens: State champions can be found in the courtyard of the Waring House. Younger specimens can be found in the Rock Alpine Garden.

Curly-Leaf Mountain Mahogany

Cercocarpus ledifolius Nutt. ex Torr. & A. Gray
Rosaceae

1 cm

By *Maria Bumgarner,* Senior Horticulturist, Denver Botanic Gardens

Cercocarpus ledifolius is a prominent shrub in the Colorado landscape. It is found in sunny areas of the Rocky Mountain steppe environment at low and middle elevations in western Colorado. It is delightful—a yellow spring bloom with one-of-a kind seedheads. The seeds resemble a small curly pipe cleaner, and one curious feature is the way they almost glow in the Colorado sun.

The history regarding Denver Botanic Gardens and the *Cercocarpus ledifolius* is also very curious. In the fall of 1971, thirty shrubs were planted throughout the Gardens. This occurred when fall plantings were rare and native plantings even rarer. Many changes have occurred over the years: seasons of drought or heavy snowfall, and entire gardens being moved. However, one of the original plants is still alive and thriving after thirty-eight years.

HEIGHT	10–15 feet
WIDTH	8–10 inches
BLOOMS	April to May (modest flowers, showy seedheads in summer)
SUN	Full sun to partial shade
SOIL MOISTURE	Xeric once established
HARDINESS	USDA zones 4b–8 (up to 7,000 feet)
CULTURE	Well-drained clay, garden loam, or sandy soil

This evergreen plant species is quite a survivor. It can be found in elevations from 4,000 to 7,000 feet; possibly lives hundreds of years; tolerates drought; and grows 4- to 12-feet tall and wide. Technically it is an angiosperm and in the rose family (Rosaceae). Throughout the winter, bright green curly leaves contrast against gray smooth bark—hence the common name of curly-leaf mountain mahogany.

The unique features of the mountain mahogany suggested the use of this shrub as the main hedge at Centennial Gardens. In 2001, Centennial Gardens became the first water-smart formal garden. This 5-acre

garden contains over 300 *Cercocarpus ledifolius* in a groomed 24-inch hedge. This native hedge has developed into a unique beauty. It requires less pruning sessions and strikes many of us as far superior to the commonly used, water guzzling privets or boxwoods.

Besides all of these great features, *Cercocarpus ledifolius* also has an added environmental benefit—it is a nitrogen fixer. This means it has a symbiotic relationship with certain soil bacteria. These organisms form nodules on the roots of plants and fix atmospheric nitrogen. Some of the nitrogen is used for the shrubs' growth and some is added to the soil for other plants. This shrub is extremely versatile in the garden and can be used for replacing fences, espalier, or as a naturalized planting.

Location at the Gardens: Shrubs are located on the east side of the Boettcher Memorial Education Building, as well as in the Rock Alpine Garden and Dryland Mesa Garden.

Rock Clematis

Clematis columbiana (Nutt.) Torr. & A. Gray var. *tenuiloba*
(A. Gray in H. Newton & W.P. Jenney) J.S. Pringle
Ranunculaceae

ILLUSTRATION BY: Libby Kyer

Rock clematis is a creeping woody vine that is native from the foothills to the tundra of the Rocky Mountains of the United States and Canada. This plant has a rhizomatous growth habit, scrambling through the soil, and slowly moving among the rocks and screes. The tight, highly dissected foliage gets about 6 inches off the ground, and it bears 1-inch pendulous, violet-blue flowers in early to late spring. In Colorado, it can be found growing in the gravelly soils around the eastern base of Pikes Peak and in the Sangre de Cristo Mountains. It is found in great abundance around the Bighorn Mountains of Wyoming and the Black Hills area of South Dakota. In the wild I've found the largest colonies growing on open, north- and east-facing rocky, grassy slopes.

Rock clematis can be very long lived in the garden (my original plants are going on fifteen years now), are cold tolerant to zone 4, and seem to do best in a well-drained soil with some afternoon shade. Some years it comes in thick with hundreds of blooms. It is usually propagated from fresh seed that is promptly planted in the fall for spring germination. This is the perfect rock garden plant that promptly appears in the tiny crevices between rocks that were too tight to plant, thus softening and naturalizing your rock garden paradise.

Location at the Gardens: The most vigorous examples are in the Pikes Peak Trough within Wildflower Treasures, but they are also grown in the Rock Alpine Garden.

HEIGHT	2–5 inches
WIDTH	10–20 inches
BLOOMS	April to June
SUN	Full sun to partial shade
SOIL MOISTURE	Moderate
HARDINESS	USDA zones 4b–8 (up to 7,000 feet)
CULTURE	Well-drained garden loam or rock garden scree (loam and gravel mix)

Photo by Kirk Fieseler

As co-owner of Laporte Avenue Nursery in Fort Collins, Colorado (wholesaler and mail order company of rare plants), **Kirk Fieseler** has introduced dozens of native and exotic rock garden plants to general cultivation. He recently retired as lead instructor for Front Range Community College in Loveland and Fort Collins.

Hairy Clematis

Clematis hirsutissima Pursh 'Garden Club of Denver'
Ranunculaceae

By *Mike Kintgen*, Horticulturist, Denver Botanic Gardens

Clematis hirsutissima is a hardy perennial that has been grown at the Gardens since 1976. Native throughout much of the American West from the Rockies and points west, this non-vining, clump-forming perennial can be found throughout foothill and montane communities. Differing from more common garden varieties of clematis in being a non-vining herbaceous perennial (think of peonies), it is the perfect addition to the perennial border, rock garden, or native garden.

The cultivar 'Garden Club of Denver' was selected by Kirk Fieseler of Laporte Avenue Nursery in Fort Collins at the Lone Pine trailhead near Red Feather Lakes, Colorado, for its superior clumping and vigorous growth habit. In my own experience, some forms of *Clematis hirsutissima* can form slightly loose-running clumps, but *C. hirsutissima* 'Garden Club of Denver' will not run and proves to be a superior garden plant.

Nodding bell-shaped flowers in shades of blue or purple hover above finely cut foliage in mid- to late spring. Interesting foliage and, later the seedheads, give this plant interest long after the flowers have faded, usually in April and May at lower elevations. In fact, the seedheads are so noticeable that the plant is sometimes given the common name lion's beard for the fluffy white seedheads that bear some resemblance to Albert Einstein's hair.

HEIGHT	8–24 inches, taller with more water
WIDTH	8–18 inches, the drier it is, the slower it will grow
BLOOMS	April and May
SUN	Sun or part shade; if in part shade, grow dry or it will flop
SOIL MOISTURE	Moderate to Dry (very xeric once established)
HARDINESS	To USDA zone 2 (to at least 9,000 feet)
CULTURE	Clay to loam

Not nearly as particular as many vining clematis, 'Garden Club of Denver' will grow in sun or part shade and all types of soil as long as drainage is good. Part shade and a soil heavy in clay are best if you are growing it very dry. Slow to establish, like peonies, one needs to wait about two to three years for it to really kick in and get going. At lower elevations along the Front Range, it may start to go somewhat dormant in mid-July if conditions are very hot and dry. It is also a good bet for most high-elevation gardens because it's native at elevations up to 9,000 feet.

Photo by Michael Kintgen

Location at the Gardens: Look for *Clematis hirsutissima* in several cultivars and forms including 'Garden Club of Denver' in Wildflower Treasures in the west and north beds; the Ponderosa Border in the Western Panoramas; and the Rock Alpine Garden, where a specimen has been living for several decades in the middle of a Juniper.

Daphne

Daphne x transatlantica C.D. Brickell & A.R. White 'Jim's Pride'
Thymelaeaceae

Cathy Cridlebaugh

By *Alan M. Schroder,* Conservatory Horticulturist, Denver Botanic Gardens

Since 1992, Denver Botanic Gardens has been home to a *Daphne* in the Rock Alpine Garden by the name of *Daphne* x *transatlantica* 'Jim's Pride'. Located slightly south of the Cactus and Succulent House in the Rock Alpine Garden and nestled into a cozy location, this plant is a wonderful example of a beautiful and fragrant daphne. The clusters of small white fragrant flowers, in combination with its evergreen habit, make this plant a worthwhile visit all year long. This plant has proven to be a wonderful selection that's a must-have for *Daphne* lovers alike, and just one of many wonderful daphnes here at the gardens.

Daphne x *transatlantica* 'Jim's Pride', or Jim's Pride daphne, was originally thought to be just *Daphne caucasica*, but was later re-examined and renamed to what it is now. Found to be a hybrid between *Daphne caucasica* and *Daphne collina*, this plant resides in the plant family Thymelaeaceae, making up one of forty-eight genera and close to 650 species in this plant family. This hardy evergreen daphne can grow to a height of anywhere from 24 to 48 inches tall, making for a showy, low growing, and manageable specimen. Near white, to white flowers emerge in April to May, intoxicating one with a heavy and wonderful scent, and often reblooming quite heavily even after the first hard frost. This plant can grow anywhere from USDA hardiness zones 5–9 and requires partial shade to do its best, but can survive in full sun.

HEIGHT	30–48 inches
WIDTH	20–36 inches
BLOOMS	April to June, then sporadically to November
SUN	Full sun to partial shade
SOIL MOISTURE	Moderate
HARDINESS	USDA zones 4b–8 (up to 7,000 feet)
CULTURE	Well-drained garden loam or sandy soil; does not like high nitrogen fertilizer; feed sparingly.

Overwatering can sometimes be a problem and it must be planted in well-drained soil. It will not tolerate extended periods of drought. As a hybrid, *Daphne* x *transatlantica* 'Jim's Pride' will not set seed because the flowers are sterile, making vegetative cuttings the most popular method of propagation. If small showy and fragrant flowering plants are an interest of yours, *Daphne* x *transatlantica* 'Jim's Pride' is certainly one to consider.

Location at the Gardens: Plants are grown in the Rock Alpine Garden and around the Waring House.

Purple Hardy Ice Plant

Delosperma cooperi (Hook. f.) L. Bolus
Aizoaceae

© Beth Lovold

By *Panayoti Kelaidis*, Senior Curator and Director of Outreach, Denver Botanic Gardens

Delosperma cooperi originates in the foothills of the Drakensberg Mountains in the Lesotho and neighboring provinces of South Africa, especially the grassy steppe of the Orange Free State. It has been grown at Denver Botanic Gardens since 1984.

Where there's smoke, there's fire. Once the hardy yellow ice plant (*Delosperma nubigenum*) had proven itself for several years, surely there had to be some other similar plants that would be hardy? Several hundred different kinds of Mesembryanthemaceae (the ungainly name for the ice plant family now classified under family Aizoaceae) were obtained from Mesa Gardens in 1983. The far flung *Index Seminum* exchange between botanic gardens around the world yielded a number of likely candidates. In the winter of 1983–84, the Botanic Garden at Bonn, Germany, sent us a modest packet of *Delosperma cooperi*.

Seedlings germinated promptly in early spring, and were set out in late May on a sunny slope of the South Ledge in the Rock Alpine Garden (where a few of their progeny persist twenty-five summers later!). The first flowers emerged by June, and by midsummer they were covered with their hot purple magenta stars. More and more staff and visitors weighed in with "surely this can't be hardy?" and "it's growing like an annual." Come autumn, the clumps slowed down and took on purple tints (a hopeful sign). I watched them with an eagle eye their first winter. The next spring they emerged unscathed and I knew a star was born.

This low-spreading groundcover resembles sedums in its tubular succulence, but does what no sedum would dream of: a massive show of color that rivals any

HEIGHT	2–3 inches
WIDTH	15–24 inches
BLOOMS	May to October
SUN	Full sun to partial shade
SOIL MOISTURE	Moderate to xeric
HARDINESS	USDA zones 4b–8 (up to 8,000 feet)
CULTURE	Well-drained garden loam or sandy soil

annual in vigor and showiness. So quickly does this grow from seed, and so generous is its seed production, that within a few years of distribution through local nurseries and the Denver Botanic Gardens' Plant Sale, Hines Wholesale Nursery published a full-page advertisement in *American Nurseryman* touting their "new introduction," which they had obtained from a Denver customer.

D. cooperi had been a mainstay of the South African nursery industry—especially in the higher, cold Highveld—for most of the twentieth century, so Denver Botanic Gardens can be said to have discovered them, much as Columbus discovered America. And yet, displaying and distributing this plant undoubtedly hastened the worldwide popularity it enjoys today, and helped lay the groundwork for the success of Plant Select.® I have no doubt that the millions and millions of purple ice plants, growing from Alaska to Florida, from California to the New York Island, can trace their genes directly to a packet of seed received at Denver Botanic Gardens on April 24, 1984.

Location at the Gardens: Purple hardy ice plants grow in the South African Plaza, Water-Smart Garden, Rock Alpine Garden, Anna's Overlook, and many other sites around the York Street gardens.

Yellow Hardy Ice Plant

Delosperma nubigenum (Schltr.) L. Bolus
Aizoaceae

By *Edward P. Connors*

Identifying plants has always been dicey, particularly for the non-trained amateur. When I forayed into the Southern Hemisphere, (South Africa, to be precise), virtually NO genera or species' names rang clear. Oh, I had grown *Pelargonium* (geranium) for years and introduced the scented varieties into Denver Botanic Gardens' Plant Sale around 1967. At one point I had over forty-five varieties in my greenhouse. BUT, I hadn't even realized that they were indigenous to South Africa. I only knew of cycads in glass houses. I was swept away by these and the wondrous protea that I first encountered in South Africa. What kind of plantsman was I?

HEIGHT	2–3 inches
WIDTH	12–30 inches
BLOOMS	April to early June
SUN	Full sun to part shade
SOIL MOISTURE	Moderate to slightly dry
HARDINESS	USDA zones 4b–8
CULTURE	Well-drained loam or gravelly soil

Then I became aware of the *Delosperma* or 'ice plant' introduced to the Denver Botanic Gardens' Plant Sale in the mid-1980s. I bought about six South African plant identification books while in the country and they didn't agree on a proper name, not once using the terms *Delosperma* or ice plant. There was a good reason for this, as it turns out: the hardy yellow ice plant so common in Denver gardens eschews the subtropical lowlands where most South Africans garden, and it was essentially minted in horticulture here in Denver.

The plant first came to Denver Botanic Gardens as "*Mesembryanthemum* sp. Basutoland." When specimens were sent to leading ice plant experts around the world for identification by Panayoti Kelaidi and John Wurdack of the Smithsonian National Herbarium, the experts returned four different names. I was obviously not the only one confused with ice plant names!

Delosperma nubigenum or delosperma of the clouds, referring to its native sites at high altitudes (6,500 feet and higher) in Lesotho and the Drakensberg mountains of KwaZulu Natal, is the lovely yellow variety that has been introduced by Denver Botanic Gardens way back in 1980. The Irish green mats are uniquely lustrous in the summer Xeriscape,™ but equally brilliant when they turn ruby red in winter. But it is only in the last ten years that other ice plants have become popular. It has been a selective process, for many do not come back in Denver after a cold winter. But not the *D. nubigenum*, for it has become one of the most popular ice plants in Denver and across the country. This succulent is unusual for, like "Hens & Chickens" (*Sempervivum*), it grows in high, moist places and returns over the years.

Despite its arbitrary naming problems the ice plant (*Delosperma*) is here to stay and has a very good reason to be in your garden.

Location at the Gardens: Plants can be found in the Rock Alpine Garden and the South African Plaza.

Edward Connors is a Life Trustee at Denver Botanic Gardens. As chairman of the board of trustees during the crucial years when the Scientific and Cultural Facilities District was forged, Ed ensured that the Gardens was a key institution. Connors and his wife, Hope, have created a beautiful garden in Cherry Hills. As teacher at Kent Country School, Ed inspired a passion for history and art in several generations of Denver's future leaders. He has led hundreds of students and members of the Gardens on tours throughout Europe.

Fendler's Hedgehog Cactus

Echinocereus fendleri (Engelm.) F. Seitz
Cactaceae

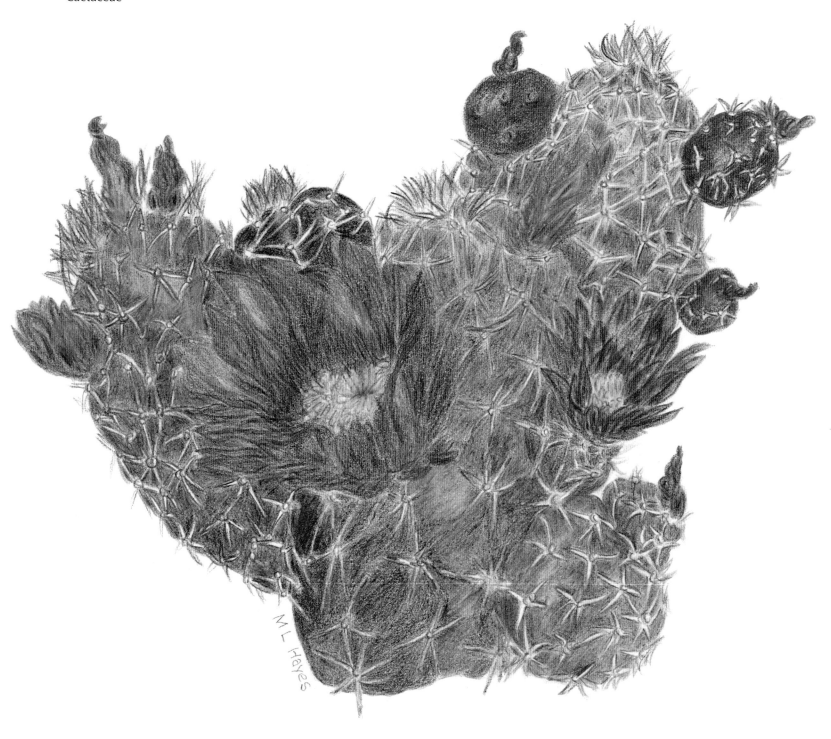

By *Jeff Ottersberg*

Fendler's hedgehog cactus grows in the southwestern United States from Texas to Arizona and southernmost Colorado, including a disjunct population near Cañon City. It is abundant throughout almost all of New Mexico and grows in northern Mexico as well.

HEIGHT	3–6 inches
WIDTH	3–5 inches
BLOOMS	May and June
SUN	Full sun
SOIL MOISTURE	Moderate to xeric
HARDINESS	USDA zones 4b–8 (up to 8,000 feet)
CULTURE	Well-drained garden loam, clay or sandy soil

The hills near La Cienaga, New Mexico (not far from Santa Fe), used to be mostly covered with blue grama grass (*Bouteloua gracilis*) and scattered single-seed junipers (*Juniperus monosperma*). In addition, I remember a wealth of beautiful wildflowers including feather dalea (*Dalea formosa*), Apache plume (*Fallugia paradoxa*), cliff fendlerbush (*Fendlera rupicola*), perkysue (*Tetraneuris argentea*), desert bluet (*Houstonia rubra*), lavender trumpet flower (*Ipomopsis longiflora*), bladderpod (*Lesquerella fendleri*), stemless evening primrose (*Oenothera caespitosa*), James' beardtongue (*Penstemon jamesii*), New Mexican bluebell (*Phacelia* sp.) and cowboy's delight (*Sphaeralcea coccinea*).

It was here that I saw my first *Echinocereus fendleri* in the wild—or perhaps anywhere. I have seen a lot of *Echinocereus fendleri* forms since then, but this one is still my favorite. The plants were scattered in the gravelly gentle slopes of the hills.

They were single stemmed, 2 to 5 inches tall (usually on the shorter side), with short, light colored curved spines. With their large purple flowers they were easy to find when in flower. When the seed was ready it was easy to collect several thousand seeds. No, I did not take them all!

I came back home, started my business in a friend's greenhouse (I had one thousand dollars) and begged, borrowed, or traded for the supplies I needed. My entrepreneurial professor said that's how you make up for the lack of money.

I don't remember how I made contact with Denver Botanic Gardens' Mother's Day Sale, but in 1992, I took some of my first crop (including Fendler's hedgehog cactus, of course) to the sale. Some of these cacti were purchased and planted at the Gardens, where they flourished. Some years later, when I ran out of seed, I was restocked with seed provided from my plants at Denver Botanic Gardens. I now have a plant grown from Denver Botanic Gardens' seed that is 8 inches tall with ten heads and slightly longer spines. Its side heads are as big as the original plants from La Cienaga. I don't know if it's a hybrid (with hybrid vigor) or just getting too much water.

Location at the Gardens: Fendler's hedgehog cactus is planted in Dryland Mesa, Wildflower Treasures, and the Rock Alpine Garden.

Jeff Ottersberg is proprietor of Wild Things, the premier wholesale grower of Great Plains and dryland Rocky Mountain native plants. He has perfected the culture of many native ball cacti, which he sells throughout the region, helping obviate the need for these to be collected in the wild in the future.

Cutleaf Fleabane

Erigeron compositus Pursh
Asteraceae

By *Ross Shrigley*, Horticulturist, Denver Botanic Gardens

*Erigeron compositu*s is commonly known as cutleaf fleabane or cutleaf daisy. It is a small native perennial that grows from Alaska to Greenland in the high montane and subalpine regions of the western mountains south to Arizona. When grown at lower elevations (zones 3–9) the small daisy-like flowers emerge in early May, about 2 to 8 inches above the clumping silver-green compound basal leaves. The flowers are usually white, but can be many different hues of blue or purple.

There are two significantly different variations of *Erigeron compositus:* one type has large flower ray petals, while the other (*Erigeron compositus* var. *glabratus*) has minuscule ray petals around the flower. The former, being showier, has two selections on the market, a pink form and 'Red Desert'. The Red Desert cultivar (named for its place of origin in the Red Desert of Wyoming) has white flowers on 2-inch stems, while the pink form has flowers on 8-inch stems with coloring that is only slightly pink. Cutleaf daisy flower colors will vary considerably across the continent, however colors within local populations are fairly uniform because these plants are primarily apomictic. This means that pollen does not usually pollinate the ovules, but rather the ovules develop into seed by themselves.

E. compositus is a short-lived plant, but will put on a lot of viable seed every year. If one prefers to encourage the plant to bloom all summer, continue dead-

HEIGHT	10–14 inches
WIDTH	15–24 inches
BLOOMS	May to July
SUN	Full sun to partial shade
SOIL MOISTURE	Moderate to xeric once established
HARDINESS	USDA zones 3–9 (up to 10,000 feet)
CULTURE	Well-drained clay, sandy or loamy soil

Photo by Panayoti Kelaidis

heading it and provide supplemental water. Everyone loves this cute early bloomer with shimmering foliage, but most people will forget to purchase it when they visit the nursery. It tends to get lost among a display of larger showy perennials. Elevated attention toward *Erigeron compositus* has made this charming plant more readily available on the market.

Location at the Gardens: Denver Botanic Gardens began displaying this plant *en masse* in the Rock Alpine Garden in 1980, and also implemented them in Wildflower Treasures starting in 2000.

Sulphur Flower

Eriogonum umbellatum Torr.
Polygonaceae

By *Maria Bumgarner*, Senior Horticulturist, Denver Botanic Gardens

Eriogonum umbellatum is a fascinating native plant that is loved for its variability. It is found from the Sierra Cascade crest to the Great Plains to central Canada. Dozens of botanical varieties have been described, varying from tiny groundcovers to small shrubs. *Eriogonum umbellatum* is part of the buckwheat family—Polygonaceae. Its common name is sulphur flower because the flower looks like a sulfur crystal. The flower blooms May through August and has the ability to be bright yellow or cream-colored. As the flower ages it can take on a variety of hues, from russet to bright red, or possibly purple.

The flower also attracts several butterflies, including the cythera metalmark, Rocky Mountain dotted blue, and the lupine blue. In 1980, the first planting of *Eriogonum umbellatum* took place in the Rock Alpine Garden. The plant was collected in Wyoming by the Gardens' Panayoti Kelaidis. It always was a gorgeous native plant and has now become a favorite in the Gardens.

HEIGHT	10–14 inches
WIDTH	15–24 inches
BLOOMS	May to July
SUN	Full sun to partial shade
SOIL MOISTURE	Moderate to xeric once established
HARDINESS	USDA zones 3–9 (up to 10,000 feet)
CULTURE	Well-drained clay, sandy or loamy soil

Erigonum umbellatum can be dead-headed after the flowers are spent and pruned for shape. This will help to show off the colorful foliage, which turns a bright red color in the fall and persisting into winter. In the last twenty-eight years, this plant has really exploded into a favorite design attraction with its formal character, drought tolerance, and butterfly magnetism.

Location at the Gardens: Groupings of this species are throughout the Gardens. Plant breeders have had fun in developing new cultivars, which can specifically be experienced in the Water-Smart Garden and Rock Alpine Garden.

Clown Fig

Ficus aspera Forster f.

By *Luke R. Tembrock*, Horticulturist, Denver Botanic Gardens

A visitor to Denver Botanic Gardens is apt to notice our only specimen of *Ficus aspera* in the southwest corner of the Boettcher Memorial Tropical Conservatory. It has reached the average height for this species—about 20 feet—and is cloaked in conspicuously variegated leaves and fruits. The almost absurd coloration of *F. aspera* leaves has given this species the common name of clown fig.

As is evident in its common name, *Ficus aspera* is in the genus commonly referred to as the figs. The figs are a large (800+ species) and diverse genus displaying growth habits similar to epiphytes, lithophytes, vines, trees, and shrubs. However, the common trait linking all figs is the mechanism by which they sexually reproduce. Figs, often thought of as fruits, are in fact flowers that have folded into orbicular shapes (technically known as a syconium) enclosing tiny flower parts. This method of hiding away the flowers may seem like an ineffective way of ensuring pollination, but the fig flower is the product of an elegant interplay between plant and insect.

Ficus syconia are in fact, wasp nurseries. Pregnant wasps fly between fig flowers trying to find the best location to lay their eggs, and in doing so, transfer pollen from one flower to another. Infant wasps are born into an ideal environment with ample food and shelter, ensuring that they will become adults and pollinate the next generation of figs. Every species of *Ficus* has its own species of wasp that pollinates it, therefore the nearly 900 species of figs are dependant upon nearly 900 species of fig wasps.

Denver Botanic Gardens acquired its *Ficus aspera* specimen in 1965, the year the conservatory construction was completed, most likely as a young tree only a few feet tall. In 1997, when the conservatory underwent remodeling and repair, all plants had to be removed from the conservatory. Since the *Ficus aspera* was a large tree, it would have been impossible to move the specimen without killing it. Therefore, a method of propagation known as air layering (wrapping a stem on a tree with moss and plastic to cause root growth) was employed to save the tree. Of course this meant that when the conservatory was replanted in 1997, *Ficus aspera* was again a small a specimen.

Keeping plants alive in this way for many years is the main goal, and also the challenge, for horticulturists at Denver Botanic Gardens. Reproducing *Ficus aspera* from seed is a particular challenge because we do not possess the wasp species from the Pacific islands where *Ficus aspera* is native. However, keeping tropical figs in our collection on a long-term basis could later be invaluable. Imagine how important our specimen would be if the wasp that pollinates *Ficus aspera* became extinct.

Location at the Gardens: The only specimen of *Ficus aspera* is in the southwest corner of the Boettcher Memorial Tropical Conservatory.

HEIGHT	Small tree to 25 feet—can be pruned to accommodate home or sunroom culture
WIDTH	10–15 feet
BLOOMS	Year round, but heaviest in spring
SUN	Full sun to partial shade
SOIL MOISTURE	Drought tolerant but prefers even moisture
HARDINESS	Tender tropical plant—protect from any frost
CULTURE	As with most ficus species, *Ficus aspera* is adaptive to a range of conditions, making them good choices for house plants.

Ashy silktassel

Garrya flavescens S. Wats.
Garryaceae

SARA-LOU KLEIN ©2008

By *Dr. Allan R. Taylor*

Garrya flavescens has several common names, such as ashy silktassel, yellow silktassel, and quinine bush. It is one of some eighteen species belonging to the genus *Garrya*, and to the family Garryaceae. This family is exclusively American, being widely distributed in western North America (including Mexico), Central America, and the Caribbean. *Garrya* species are dioecious—having separate male and female individuals.

All of the *Garrya* species are evergreen shrubs or small trees, varying in height from 3 to 15 feet. The leaves of plants in the family Garryaceae occur in opposite pairs and are simple, leathery, dark green to gray-green, and elliptic, with an entire margin and a short petiole. The flowers of the family Garryaceae are catkin-like inflorescences grouped in pendulous clusters, the staminate and pistillate flowers differing somewhat in structure. The flowers are wind-pollinated. The catkins are produced during the spring and summer, but attain full growth and sexual maturity in the late winter. The fruit is produced by the female plant, and is a round dry drupe containing two seeds.

HEIGHT	6–8 feet
WIDTH	4–6 feet
BLOOMS	March to May
SUN	Full sun to partial shade
SOIL MOISTURE	Moderate to xeric once established
HARDINESS	USDA zones 5–9 (up to 6,000 feet)
CULTURE	Well drained clay, sandy or loamy soil

The hardiest members of the genus are *Garrya flavescens*, *G. ovata*, and *G. wrightii*, and of these, the most hardy is *G. flavescens*, the subject of this description.

Garrya flavescens has a natural range that includes the more southern parts of California, Nevada, Arizona, New Mexico, and Utah. It is an extremely drought-tolerant shrub, around 6 to 8 feet tall when mature, with gray-green (sometimes yellowish) leathery, evergreen leaves that are longer than they are wide. The grayish cast to the leaves is caused by the presence of silky hairs on both leaf surfaces; the small fruits are also covered with white silky hairs. The leaves and twigs have a bitter taste, hence the common name "quinine bush."

The plant is found in desert, chaparral, and dry forest (piñon-juniper and ponderosa pine) habitats from 2,500 to 7,000 feet above sea level. Some individuals are hardy to at least –20° F. (USDA zone 5), and possibly more. Good places to view the plant in nature are Oak Creek Canyon, south of Flagstaff, Arizona, or Zion National Park in Utah, (near the Golob exit from I-15).

The largest *Garrya flavescens* in the collection of Denver Botanic Gardens is currently around 7 feet tall and was planted in 1981. The plant is probably female

and produces its catkins in late winter or early spring (February–April). It cannot reproduce due to the absence in the Gardens of another mature *Garrya flavescens* of the opposite sex.

This strikingly beautiful shrub is easy to cultivate: it prefers spare, well-drained soil, and requires little supplemental watering. It is an ideal plant for xeriscape plantings. Propagation of *G. flavescens* can be somewhat difficult. Seedlings damp off very easily; the seed should be sown in a sterile medium and watered sparingly, and kept in bright light—sunlight if possible.

Garrya flavescens also can be propagated by cutting, although the percentage actually striking roots is usually extremely low. Hardwood cuttings of last season's growth, treated with rooting hormone, are inserted into a medium kept lightly moist, either by intermittent mist or irrigation. Rooting is promoted by bottom heat. The beauty of the ashy silktassel justifies all of the toil and precautions necessary to produce a growing specimen, however, and the reward in the garden can not be over estimated: the paucity of hardy broad-leafed evergreen shrubs and trees in our area makes them invaluable, and *Garrya flavescens* is among the very best.

Location at the Gardens: The largest *Garrya flavescens* is growing in the Rock Alpine Garden on the right side of the path just to the north of the Cactus and Succulent House. There are also young specimens in the Watersmart Garden and the Rock Alpine Garden.

Dr. Taylor is a retired professor of Linguistics at the University of Colorado in Boulder, and a lifelong horticulturist with extensive field knowledge and experience growing hundreds of western native plants. He is on the board of the International Oak Society.

Hardy Gazania

Gazania linearis (Thunb.) Druce and *Gazania krebsiana* Less.
Asteraceae

ILLUSTRATION BY: Sylvia Johnson

By *Panayoti Kelaidis*, Senior Curator and Director of Outreach, Denver Botanic Gardens

Once several kinds of ice plants proved to be very winter hardy, why not expand the scope and see if other South African plants might not join their ranks? In the mid-1980s, I had heard that Ken and Leslie Gillanders were traveling to the Drakensberg mountains to explore and collect seed. They proffered us some samples, and the first to germinate and bloom was a brilliant yellow gazania with linear, dark green leaves. This bloomed a few months after sowing in early spring, producing masses of flowers throughout the summer months and into winter. I expected the plant to succumb (surely gazanias can't be winter hardy!), but not only did it persist in the coldest months, it continued putting out the occasional blossom during warm spells in the winter.

I made a point of collecting seed of every high-altitude form of *Gazania linearis* I could find on my 1994 expedition to South Africa. This is the only species to occur at high elevations in the Drakensberg, but is very variable in size, spotting on the flowers, and vigor. Planted near one another, these various accessions obviously began to intergrade, leading to Colorado Gold,™ a wonderfully vigorous strain debuted by Plant Select® in 1998. This strain is now grown and sold by nurseries across the United States. It has proven very hardy at higher altitudes in Colorado by thriving at Betty Ford Alpine Gardens at over 8,000 feet. It can produce abundant seedlings in optimal conditions, but these are easily removed.

HEIGHT	3–5 inches
WIDTH	10–12 inches
BLOOMS	April to May peak, then in flushes throughout the growing season
SUN	Full sun to partial shade
SOIL MOISTURE	Moderate watering to dry
HARDINESS	USDA zones 4–8 (up to 9,000 feet)
CULTURE	Thrives in loam; needs light fertilizing in sandy soils

In 2003, *Gazania linearis* was joined by *Gazania krebsiana* Tanager,™ a neon orange cousin with more deeply divided foliage, originating at lower elevations in semiarid South African karoo. It is not as cold hardy, but is even more drought and heat tolerant than its yellow cousin. Sahin Seed Company in the Netherlands gave Plant Select® permission to trademark 'Orange Peacock' as Tanager,™ a selection made by Kees Sahin from seed he had obtained from Kirstenbosch in 1975. This, too, has become very popular since it was promoted by Plant Select.® Both gazanias are essentially ever-blooming perennials for xeriscapes, rock gardens, and informal perennial beds. Their blossoms are never more welcome than in the depths of winter, when they are wont to produce the random, rogue flower.

Location at the Gardens: Plants can be found in the South African Plaza, Rock Alpine Garden, Water-Smart Garden, Waring House Garden, El Pomar Waterway, and many more gardens throughout Denver.

Red Flowered False Yucca, Red Yucca, Texas Red Yucca

Hesperaloe parviflora (Torr.) J.M. Coult.
Agavaceae

ILLUSTRATION BY: Mervi Hjelmroos-Koski

By *Dan Johnson*, Associate Director of Horticulture & Curator of Native Plants, Denver Botanic Gardens

60

There are many species of *Hesperaloe* found in Mexico and scattered in west central Texas, especially the Edwards Plateau. This one has been a standard of gardeners in the Southwest for many decades, as it should be, but the notion that they would survive a Colorado winter was suspect, to say the least. In 1985, they appeared at Paulino Gardens, a local nursery, and an optimistic Gayle Weinstein, Director of Horticulture for Denver Botanic Gardens at the time, thought we should try them. Thanks, Gayle! This might have taken a few more decades to discover otherwise. They thrive in sun and heat, and prefer to be dry, especially through the winter months. Not a bad combination!

Though this is called a red yucca, it is not a true yucca—yet it is related. Long deep green leaves are nearly cylindrical with a long groove down the length, and they form a gracefully arching rosette. Flowering

HEIGHT	4–7 feet
WIDTH	18–30 inches
BLOOMS	May to October
SUN	Full sun
SOIL MOISTURE	Moderate to xeric
HARDINESS	USDA zones 4b–8 (up to 6,000 feet)
CULTURE	Well-drained clay, sandy soil or loam

stems rise quickly in the spring, and here is where they out-perform any yucca: the stems that appear in spring continue to flower all summer long, making true yuccas seem like a flash in the pan. Stems can rise to 5 or 6 feet tall, clothed in tropical coral-red and yellow flowers that will lure hummingbirds from your neighbors' gardens into yours. Seed pods are common and interesting in the winter landscape.

Location at the Gardens: These plants can be found in the Water-Smart Garden and the Dryland Mesa Garden.

Orange Sneezeweed, Owl's-Claws

Hymenoxys hoopesii (A. Gray) Bierner
Synonyms: *Helenium hoopesii* A. Gray,
Dugaldia hoopesii (A. Gray) Rydb.
Asteraceae

By *Michael Bone,* Senior Horticulturist, Greenhouse and Propagation, Denver Botanic Gardens

62

Hymenoxys hoopesii can be found throughout the Colorado Rockies, Sierra Nevadas, Cascades, and in many pine forests throughout the West. In Colorado, it is commonly found at the edge of ponderosa, bristlecone, aspen, and lodgepole pine forests, typically in clearings and high elevation meadows.

The oldest accession in Denver Botanic Gardens is from 1983, and the seed reportedly came from the Beijing Botanic Garden. Introduction from a Chinese source is unusual because this is one of the dominant yellow composite flowers found in the western part of the United States at elevations above 8,500 feet. The oldest herbarium specimen is from 1938, however, it is from a donated collection of plants. The oldest specimen *collected* for Denver Botanic Gardens records is from July 3, 1955, from "open hillsides in Gunnison County." *H. hoopesii* makes a valuable addition to native and xeric landscapes, but it is versatile enough to add height and interest to any garden. Plants have long strap-like leaves that can be covered in a waxy coating, making the basal rosettes almost blue.

HEIGHT	24–36 inches
WIDTH	10–15 inches
BLOOMS	June to July
SUN	Partial shade or cool sun
SOIL MOISTURE	Moderate
HARDINESS	USDA zones 3–8 (up to 10,000 feet)
CULTURE	Garden loam or sandy soils are best

Like many high-elevation plants, when grown at lower elevations, plants often get much larger than you would see in their natural setting. Here in Denver, flower stalks can reach $2\frac{1}{2}$ to 3 inches tall. The bright yellow flowers tower above many of our shorter early spring flowers, which help soften and smooth out some of the intensity of other, more garish spring colors. As they fade and begin to set seed, the plants are left with a nice fuzzy, puffy seedhead. Plants

do go summer dormant, giving room to over-plant with heat-loving annuals, or a late-to-emerge woody legume.

As we progress further into the palette of native dry-loving garden plants, *H. hoopesii* was one of the first, and is still one of the most versatile of Colorado's wild flowers to be taken to the mainstream of local horticulture.

One interesting sidelight on this plant is its photo-toxicity to albino animals: sheep in particular can be poisoned if they eat large quantities of sneezeweed. Needless to say, sheep ranchers are not enamored of this beautiful native daisy. Don't let Fido nibble sneezeweed if he has white fur!

Location at the Gardens: H. hoopesii is grown mainly in the Sacred Earth Garden. It can also be found in Dryland Mesa, the Rock Alpine Garden, Wildflower Treasures, and the Ponderosa and Bristlecone Borders of Western Panoramas.

Tall Bearded Iris

Iris 'Ruth Porter Waring'
Iridaceae

By *Ann Montague*, Gardener, Denver Botanic Gardens

64

In 1988, iris hybridizer John Durrance introduced a new iris to the public. He described it in that spring's edition of the American Iris Society Bulletin as follows:

> *A brown rose-red self with ruffled and laced falls. Named for Aunt Ruth, a 98-year-old lady who is a true garden lover and a long time friend. A loyal supporter of our flower, member of AIS, and lifetime board member of the Denver Botanic Gardens. Her favorite color is red.*

Medicine brought John Durrance to Colorado—he was awarded an internship with an internationally known expert on tuberculosis, Dr. James J. Waring, co-founder of the Webb-Waring Institute at the University of Colorado. As a specialist in pulmonary medicine, Durrance became head of the pulmonary department at the Denver veterans' hospital.

While medicine was his vocation, his avocation was flower hybridization—gladiolus, tulips, and finally, iris. Seventy of his iris hybridizations, among them numerous award winners, were registered with the American Iris Society from the 1950s until his death in 2003. One of his creations, a beautiful ruffled red iris, he named for his friend and fellow Denver Botanic Gardens' trustee, Ruth Porter Waring.

HEIGHT	30–50 inches
WIDTH	10–30 inches
BLOOMS	May and June
SUN	Full sun to partial shade
SOIL MOISTURE	Moderate
HARDINESS	USDA zones 4b–8 (up to 7,000 feet)
CULTURE	Well-drained garden loam

A true "self" with the fuzzy beard matching the petal color, *Iris* 'Ruth Porter Waring' has rose-red standards (upper petals) and falls (lower petals). Both the standards and falls have ruffled edges; the edges of the falls are tightly ruffled giving them a lacy look. Topping 27½ inches tall from base to top of flower stalk, it is classified as a tall bearded iris. This hybrid resulted from a cross between *Iris* 'Mulled Wine', a raspberry burgundy flower and *Iris* 'Palmer Leader', which has a ruffled red flower with a bronze red beard. In Denver it typically blooms around Memorial Day, mid-season for irises.

Named for the Greek goddess of the rainbow, references to irises have been woven into art and literature for centuries, from the writings and art of ancient Greece, to the stylized flower in the French fleur-de-lis, to carvings in India's great Taj Mahal. With hundreds of species, and native habitats ranging from marshy stream edges to hot, dry deserts of the Middle East, irises are found in the wild in most temperate countries of the Northern Hemisphere. These native (*or* species) irises are the foundation for today's spectacular hybrids. While irises have been in cultivation for centuries, true hybridization programs did not begin until the latter part of the nineteenth century. Today there are thousands of hybrids in cultivation.

Of all iris species, tall bearded irises are among the most familiar to Denver's gardeners. Well adapted to our sunny, semi-arid climate and requiring a minimum of care, tall bearded irises can be counted on to provide tall, regal flowers each year. They typically bloom from late May through mid-June, depending on the cultivar. After blooming, their sword-like foliage provides a bold contrast to companion plantings throughout the growing season.

Location at the Gardens: This iris is located in the Lilac Garden and the O'Fallon Perennial Border.

Little Walnut

Juglans microcarpa Berl.
Juglandaceae

By *Michael Bone,* Senior Horticulturist, Greenhouse and Propagation, Denver Botanic Gardens

Little walnut, native to the south-central portions of the United States, including Texas, Oklahoma, Kansas, and New Mexico, makes a great addition to the palette of woody shrubs that can be used in almost any garden situation. It is surprising that these plants have not been found in the wild within Colorado's borders. The Gardens' tree was planted in June of 1986, and has since been measured as the state champion. Plantsman, propagator, and native plant expert, Jim Borland, has collected seed from plants less than 10 miles from the Colorado border in a state park in Oklahoma. With such close proximity, one could imagine that there might yet be an undiscovered population in the canyonlands of the southeastern portion of the state.

J. microcarpa has thick leathery pinnate leaves that shine and glimmer on bright summer days. Plants are small trees or large shrubs reaching about 18 feet high and 10 feet wide at maturity. A single plant can produce hundreds of seeds—about half the size of walnuts—which are a delicacy to the North American squirrel. One day, a very dedicated seed collector named Katy Wilcox was trying to gather as many seeds from the plant in June's PlantAsia as she could before the squirrels got them all. The squirrels were so angry with her for taking one of their favorite meals that they would charge down the branches barking like dogs, physically throwing seeds, trying desperately to chase her away. Her persistence paid off and we got most of the seed, but at a pretty high cost. I had never seen anything quite as ridiculous as that terrible display of poorly behaved squirrels.

Seeds are not only important to the rodents; the fleshy outer coating also creates a very strong black dye, staining skin, clothes, tools, and everything that comes near it for a very long time. It was used by indigenous people to color blankets, pottery, and clothing.

HEIGHT	10–18 feet
WIDTH	8–12 feet
BLOOMS	April (inconspicuous), fruit early September
SUN	Full sun to partial shade
SOIL MOISTURE	Xeric once established
HARDINESS	USDA zones 4–9 (up to 7,000 feet)
CULTURE	Well-drained garden loam, clay or sand

Location at the Gardens: These shrubs can be found growing in June's PlantAsia (Colorado State Champion specimen) and the Rock Alpine Garden.

Torch Lily

Kniphofia caulescens Baker ex Hook. f.
(pronounced with a hard "k"—k-nee-POFF-ee-a,
in honor of the German professor of medicine and
botanist Johannes Kniphof who pronounced
his name this way)
Asphodelaceae

ILLUSTRATION BY: Maria J. Ramsdale

Maria J Ramsdale

By *Lauren Springer Ogden*

A flower grows amid windblown grasses in the mountains of eastern South Africa. The nearest tree may be miles away; the nearest forest, even farther. A sunbird, an iridescent pollinator similar to the hummingbird of the Americas, searches for nectar, its eyes drawn to bright reds and oranges. How do bird and flower come together over this vast, grassy sea of seeming sameness?

The uniquely flashy flower spikes of *Kniphofia caulescens* and *Kniphofia triangularis* (shown on page 71–72), with their fiery orange, yellow, and/or coral tubular flowers, are carried high above their foliage on thick, wind-resistant, bird-perchable stems—waving bird beacons in the wild meadows of their homeland. They draw plant-smitten people the same way: It's virtually impossible to ignore a plant so obvious, singular, and eye-catching.

HEIGHT	20–36 inches
WIDTH	18–24 inches
BLOOMS	August to October
SUN	Full sun to partial shade
SOIL MOISTURE	Moderate
HARDINESS	USDA zones 4b–8 (up to 7,000 feet)
CULTURE	Well-drained garden loam

Kniphofia, known also as red-hot poker and tritoma, is an African genus of about seventy species of herbaceous perennials in the family Asphodelaceae (Asphodel family), closely allied to the very similar yet succulent aloes that hark from drier, less temperate regions of the same continent. *Kniphofia* species grow mainly in mountainous and moist places, and a few have been cultivated in Europe and in Africa by Caucasian settlers for three centuries. Native peoples grew and enjoyed them long before that. The Basuto, living in the Drakensberg (a north-south oriented high mountain range in the eastern part of southern Africa), traditionally plant *Kniphofia caulescens* next to their homes as a charm to protect from frequent lightning.

In Colorado a large, coarse-stemmed, orange and yellow species labeled *Kniphofia uvaria* was for many years the only dependably hardy selection of the genus grown. It is actually *K. baurii*, and it blooms in early summer for a short period. More refined hybrids and species common in gardens of milder winter climates had not fared well. When Panayoti Kelaidis of Denver Botanic Gardens made his groundbreaking first botanical foray into southern Africa in 1994, he brought back seed of several species of *Kniphofia*, some new to cultivation. He continued to bring more on successive trips, and trialed them at the Gardens, sharing seed with local, national, and international plantspeople, as he is known to do with his myriad plant acquisitions and introductions.

Thanks to the work at Denver Botanic Gardens, two of the finest torch lilies for Colorado have turned

Photo by Lauren S. Ogden

out to be *Kniphofia triangularis* and *K. caulescens*, the latter introduced to American horticulture via Seneca Hill nursery in Oswego, New York, with plants grown from Kelaidis' seed. Both are semi-evergreen depending on snow cover, winter winds, and cold, and both bloom in late summer and autumn, a real boon to sagging post-June gardens.

K. caulescens is altogether a larger, coarser plant, 20 to 36 inches tall in bloom, with the best foliage of the genus. Stemmed (hence the specific epithet *caulescens*) rosettes of wide, triangularly keeled, stiff, glaucous leaves sit like giant turquoise starfish in the garden. Thick, asparagus-like flower buds thrust from the rosettes in July and August in the northern hemisphere. Coral buds open—the lower flowers first—turning a pale creamy yellow, with spidery stamens protruding from the tubes, making a bushy, bi-colored spike.

I had the pleasure of seeing acre-wide colonies of this plant blooming in seasonally wet, grassy meadows at about 9,000 feet elevation in the southern Drakensberg, with a shimmering entourage of metallic green sunbirds drinking their nectar. Though semi-aquatic and growing in somewhat peaty soil in the wild, this plant has adapted to alkaline clay soils with much less water in Colorado. The characteristic thick rhizomes and fleshy roots and foliage of the genus may account for the plants' adaptability to less moisture away from their native haunts.

K. caulescens is dependably hardy to USDA zone 5a without snow cover, and, unlike a number of other southern African plants, seems to enjoy snow. Plants thrive on weekly water during the growing season in Colorado, with no other demands but full sun. On one of our trips to Africa, my husband found an unusual individual that was entirely yellow. It would be interesting to propagate single-colored selections from the wild, as many people find them even more attractive and easier to integrate visually into a garden.

Location at the Gardens: *Kniphofia* species and hybrids grow in many areas of the Gardens. The South African Plaza showcases the two species discussed here, amid grasses from the same region. I designed the original version of this garden, placing Colorado sandstone slabs vertically as a backdrop to call forth the cave sandstone of the Drakensberg foothills where many *Kniphofia* and beautiful grasses flourish.

Lauren Springer Ogden designs gardens nationally with her husband Scott Ogden, and has authored four horticultural books. She designed the Water-Smart Garden, Fragrance Garden, and Schlessman Plaza at Denver Botanic Gardens, along with parts of the O'Fallon Perennial Walk and South African Plaza, and has taught at Denver Botanic Gardens since 1991.

Torch Lily

Kniphofia triangularis Kunth

By *Lauren Springer Ogden*

72

Kniphofia triangularis is a demure species, and my favorite of the genus. (I've grown more than forty species and hybrids of *Kniphofia*, and killed many over my twenty winters gardening here.) It has the same cultural adaptations and limitations as its coarser cousin. The plant rarely grows much taller than 12 to 18 inches, and the narrow, lax foliage resembles a tussock of deep green grass. The flower spikes have a triangular top, hence the botanical name. Buds and mature flowers are shades of the same color, rare in the genus. They range from tangerine to coral to red.

HEIGHT	15–20 inches
WIDTH	10–15 inches
BLOOMS	August to October
SUN	Full sun to partial shade
SOIL MOISTURE	Moderate
HARDINESS	USDA zones 4b–8 (up to 7,000 feet)
CULTURE	Well-drained garden loam

Plants bloom for two months, starting in August, and would go on even longer if hard frosts didn't cut them short.

I also enjoyed this plant *in situ* in southern Africa on slightly drier, steeper slopes of the south Drakensberg as solitary plants amid grasses, and as large, showy groups in moist grassland in the lower, milder winter and hotter summer Amatola mountains of the East Cape Province. The flowers glow in a way I've only seen as a child walking railroad tracks in New Jersey spotting orange *Asclepias tuberosa*, our splendid native butterfly weed.

K. triangularis' smaller size and finer texture allow it a wider range of design possibilities than its drama-queen cousin *K. caulescens*. Both plants look superb

Photo by Lauren S. Ogden

with grasses, whether incorporated into a mesic meadow matrix or planted with specimen grasses. In Colorado I grow them with airy, wild-looking plants that play off their show-stopping, exotic looks—*Eryngium planum*, *Verbena bonariensis,* and bronze fennel are some of my favorite non-grassy companions, attracting bees, butterflies, and non-aggressive wasps. Hummingbirds vie for the *Kniphofia* flowers; I cut one or two for the vase, where they last well over a week.

Here in Colorado, because Panayoti Kelaidis and Denver Botanic Gardens opened the horticultural door to hardy southern African plants, new *Kniphofia* grow and glow. Adaptable and non-invasive, these plants deserve a place in the global garden. Growing *Kniphofia* allow gardeners, farmers of beauty that we are, to enjoy a bit of the exotic magic of southern Africa along with our native hummingbirds.

Location at the Gardens: *Kniphofia* species and hybrids grow in many areas of the Gardens. The South African Plaza showcases the two species discussed here, amid grasses from the same region. I designed the original version of this garden, placing Colorado sandstone slabs vertically as a backdrop to call forth the cave sandstone of the Drakensberg foothills where many *Kniphofia* and beautiful grasses flourish.

Lauren Springer Ogden designs gardens nationally with her husband Scott Ogden, and has authored four horticultural books. She designed the Water-Smart Garden, Fragrance Garden, and Schlessman Plaza at Denver Botanic Gardens, along with parts of the O'Fallon Perennial Walk and South African Plaza, and has taught at Denver Botanic Gardens since 1991.

BIBLIOGRAPHY FOR PAGES 69–73

Codd, L.E. *The South African Species of Kniphofia.* Bothalia, vol. 9, parts 3 & 4. Botanical Research Institute, Pretoria, RSA: October 1969.

Manning, John. *Eastern Cape South African Wildflower Guide 11.* Botanical Society of South Africa in association with the National Botanical Institute. NBD/Paarl Print, Cape Town, RSA: 2001.

Pooley, Elsa. *Mountain Flowers: A Field Guide to the Flora of the Drakensberg and Lesotho.* The Flora Publications Trust c/o National Herbarium, Durban, RSA: 2003.

Dotted Gayfeather, Snakeroot

Liatris punctata
Asteraceae

Joan Patten Kind

By *Maria Bumgarner,* Senior Horticulturist, Denver Botanic Gardens

Liatris punctata is the only truly xeric species of *Liatris*. It is native to most of the Great Plains in hot, dry, open spaces. It was donated to the Denver Botanic Gardens in 1979 by Paul Maslin, who led many plant-finding tours for the Gardens. He was a professor of biology at the University of Colorado and a great inspiration to those who knew him. Over the last thirty years, *Liatris punctata* has become a popular landscape plant and a solid performer in a variety of xeric gardens.

Currently, there is a grouping of *Liatris punctata* next to the Rock Alpine Garden and Gates Montane Pond that has survived since 1981. This species of *Liatris* can grow in a variety of soils, is hardy to zone 4 and has many benefits in the garden. It is deer resistant, a food source for birds, a popular cut flower, and an excellent source of nectar for a variety of butterflies. The endangered Pawnee montane skipper butterfly, *Hesperia leonardus* var. *montana,* is dependent upon *Liatris* populations for feeding. *Liatris* blooms from July to September and has unique fluffy brown seed spikes throughout the winter.

Besides being a great plant and easy to grow, *Liatris punctata* also has a unique medical history. It was a popular herb with several Native American tribes. The roots were known to have the ability to cure a variety of ailments, from nosebleeds to digestive diseases. However, the most popular medicinal use was its ability to treat snakebites. Consequently, it is often referred to as snakeroot.

HEIGHT	10–20 inches
WIDTH	5–12 inches
BLOOMS	July to September
SUN	Full sun to partial shade
SOIL MOISTURE	No irrigation needed once established
HARDINESS	USDA zones 4–8 (up to 9,000 feet)
CULTURE	Well-drained garden loam, clay or sand

Location at the Gardens: In addition to the Rock Alpine Garden and Gates Montane Pond, this species is also grown in Wildflower Treasures and the Laura Smith Porter Plains Garden.

Frémont's Barberry

Mahonia fremontii (Torr.) Fedde
Synonym: *Berberis fremontii* Torr.
Berberidaceae

By *Scott Skogerboe*

Frémont's barberry is native to the American Southwest in the grasslands and piñon/juniper uplands of eastern California, northern Arizona, southern Nevada, northern New Mexico, southeastern Utah, and west-central Colorado. It has been grown at the Denver Botanic Gardens since 1982. This shrub is named after General John Charles Frémont, who led two expeditions to California in the 1840s. Frémont has the distinction of being the first botanical collector of the Sierra Nevada, and was the first senator from California. He also ran unsuccessfully as the Republican candidate for president in 1856.

Frémont's barberry is one of our most spectacular and underutilized native broadleaf evergreen shrubs. Smaller in stature than its cousin, the red barberry (*Mahonia haematocarpa*), it usually grows between 5 and 10 feet tall and wide. It also has a more northerly native range. The pinnate compound foliage has a handsome bluish-green color, taking on an even more enhanced bluish-purple tone in winter. The abundant sweetly fragrant bright yellow flowers open in large clusters in late spring. The dry inflated fruits that form in mid-August are usually blue, but on occasion yellow, and red-fruited forms have been observed in nature. In our dry western climate it is hardy to zone 5.

HEIGHT	5–10 feet
WIDTH	5–6 feet
BLOOMS	April
SUN	Full sun to partial shade
SOIL MOISTURE	Xeric once established
HARDINESS	USDA zones 6–9 (up to 6,000 feet)
CULTURE	Well-drained garden loam, clay or sand

As noted earlier, the Frémont barberry is underutilized in the landscape. The reason for this is because it is difficult to propagate and grow in the nursery. Like the red barberry, it is a very slow grower early in life and doesn't thrive in container culture. As a result, both are relatively hard to find. If you see one at your favorite garden center don't hesitate to snap it up, even if it looks puny, because it won't be there for long.

Frémont's barberry performs best in perfectly drained soils that are kept on the dry side. Once established in the xeric garden, it will quickly return to a state of health and provide you with years of beauty and enjoyment. Just a word of caution: the leaves are tipped with stickers, so be sure to wear gloves when gardening near this shrub.

Location at the Gardens: Plants are grown in Dryland Mesa and the Rock Alpine Garden.

Scott Skogerboe is propagator at Fort Collins Wholesale Nursery. Scott, along with Gary Epstein, has introduced a suite of outstanding new woody plants to Colorado. Scott cracked the secrets of propagating our Rocky Mountain manzanitas, and is an authority on the plants of the USDA Cheyenne Experiment Station, which is now a satellite of the Cheyenne Botanic Gardens.

Red Barberry

Mahonia haematocarpa (Woot.) Fedde
Synonym: *Berberis haematocarpa* Woot.
Berberidaceae

By *Scott Skogerboe*

berries are only ½ inch in diameter, they are abundant and have a pleasing flavor reminiscent of wild plums. In arid climates it is hardy to zone 5.

To grow red barberry successfully, patience is a prerequisite. Although easy to germinate, the young seedlings are slow and temperamental in the nursery. They often take two years to grow into a 2¼ inch pot. Because of this trait they are harder to find in the garden centers. When establishing it in the garden, perfect drainage is preferred. Be careful not to overwater it to avoid root rot. Although the sharp leaves make this large shrub a great protective place for birds to nest, the leaves are very prickly and slow to decompose, so wear gloves when pulling weeds underneath. But have no fear, with age, the red barberry becomes a stellar addition to the dryland garden.

Location at the Gardens: The shrub is grown in the Water-Smart Garden and Dryland Mesa.

Red barberry is native to the American Southwest from southeastern California, southern Nevada, Arizona, the southerly two-thirds of New Mexico, the Trans-Pecos of west Texas, and a disjunct population in south-central Colorado. It is also found in the Mexican states of Sonora and Chihuahua.

It has been planted at Denver Botanic Gardens since 1980. Red barberry becomes a large, rounded shrub with age, eventually reaching 12 feet tall and equally as wide. It has sharply pointed pinnate compound leaves 3 inches long and 1½ inches wide. It is a beautiful ornamental dryland shrub with sweetly fragrant showy yellow flowers in late spring, followed by vivid red juicy edible berries ripening in early to mid-August. Although the

HEIGHT	10–12 feet
WIDTH	12 feet
BLOOMS	May
SUN	Full sun to partial shade
SOIL MOISTURE	Xeric once established
HARDINESS	USDA zones 5–9 (up to 6,000 feet)
CULTURE	Well-drained garden loam, clay or sand

Scott Skogerboe is propagator at Fort Collins Wholesale Nursery. Scott, along with Gary Epstein, has introduced a suite of outstanding new woody plants to Colorado. Scott cracked the secrets of propagating our Rocky Mountain manzanitas, and is an authority on the plants of the USDA Cheyenne Experiment Station, which is now a satellite of the Cheyenne Botanic Gardens.

Roundleaf Horehound

Marrubium rotundifolium Boiss.
Lamiaceae

By *Marcia Tatroe*

When it debuted in the Water-Smart Garden in 1989, this strikingly attractive horehound became an instant sensation in the local horticultural community. From rocky slopes on Ala Dag in the Taurus Mountains of Turkey, *Marrubium rotundifolium* was introduced to Denver Botanic Gardens in 1986 as seed collected by Czech explorer Zdenek Zvolánek. While highly prized by Front Range gardeners, xeric *Marrubium rotundifolium* is still relatively obscure in other parts of the country. When you do find it mentioned at all, the common name is generally listed as either silver-edged horehound or roundleaf horehound.

A member of Lamiaceae, or mint family, *Marrubium rotundifolium* features square stems characteristic of mints. Fortunately, silver-edged horehound does not make a nuisance of itself like many of its weedier relatives. Nor does it run by rhizomes or spread by seed like the better known horehound *Marrubium vulgare*, a noxious weed in much of the United States.

Marrubium rotundifolium makes a mat 4 to 6 inches tall and 15 to 18 inches wide. Each slightly scalloped leaf is outlined in white and stands out in relief against its companions. The tops of the leaves are grayish-green, the undersides white and heavily veined. The whole plant, including stems, is covered with a thick felt. To the touch, the leaves are as soft as the inside of a kitten's ear. Evergreen, or semi-evergreen in severe winters, the semi-woody stems can be cut back nearly to the ground at any time to tidy things up or to reduce legginess.

HEIGHT	4–6 inches
WIDTH	15–18 inches
BLOOMS	May to June (modest flowers: this is a foliage plant)
SUN	Full sun to partial shade
SOIL MOISTURE	Moderate to xeric once established
HARDINESS	USDA zones 4b–8 (up to 7,000 feet)
CULTURE	Well-drained clay, garden loam or sandy soil

As perennials go, silver-edged horehound's flowers are decidedly understated—so small, in fact, you might need reading glasses to see them. But what this plant lacks in flower power it more than makes up for with elegant foliage. One growing along a path looks like a pile of dimes spilled into a pool of water.

The inconspicuous white flowers are borne in whorls on stems that stand up to 10 inches above the foliage. Many gardeners cut them off, but don't if you are trying to attract honeybees. Bees fight to collect nectar from these tiny flowers. Allowed to dry in place, seedheads become golden as they age and are quite handsome in contrast to the silvery mounds.

Eschewing hot, humid summers and damp winters, *Marrubium rotundifolium* feels right at home in Colorado. Site plants in any lean soil in full sun, and don't pamper them. Infrequent watering produces tighter mounds. Hardy to −20° F, deer and rabbits leave silver-edged horehound alone, making it an ideal choice for foothill gardens.

Savvy gardeners know that to create a really satisfying garden you must have engaging foliage as well as flowers. Few plants play as well with others as *Marrubium rotundifolium*. It is especially pleasing paired with strong vertical forms of ornamental grasses, agaves, chollas, and yuccas. But silver-edged horehound is equally effective cascading over a wall or in a rock garden. For extra impact, tuck small bulbs close in so their flowers pop up through the silvery foliage.

Location at the Gardens: Horehound is found in the Water-Smart Garden and the Rock Alpine Garden.

A leading regional authority on gardening, **Marcia Tatroe** has created a great four-season garden in Centennial. She writes for *The Denver Post, Sunset Magazine* and other national publications, and her book *Cutting Edge Gardening in the Intermountain West* was recently published.

Blackfoot Daisy, Plains Blackfoot, Rock Daisy

Melampodium leucanthum Torr. & A. Gray
Asteraceae

By *Larry Vickerman,* Director of Denver Botanic Gardens at Chatfield

The blackfoot daisy is one of my all-time favorite native perennials. A low, bushy plant (6 to 12 inches tall by same wide) that boasts numerous composite flowers of 8 to 10 white rays surrounding a yellow central disk flower, blackfoot daisy is at home in a xeric planting or rock garden. It will produce blooms throughout the summer months in even the driest and hottest parts of the growing season. The dainty flowers emit a light honey scent, which attracts bees and other insect pollinators.

A true arid-lands dweller, it is native to dry, rocky-gravelly limestone based soils ranging from southeastern Colorado and southwest Kansas, south throughout Arizona and New Mexico, the panhandle of Oklahoma, north and west Texas, and northern Mexico. The prolific flowers appear in March in the southern part of its range and June in more northerly climates. I vividly remember spotting blackfoot daisy blooming prolifically, scattered along the limestone outcroppings in southwest Kansas, even with mid-summer temperatures hovering above 100° F. Its companion plants in these windswept grasslands include prairie zinnia (*Zinnia grandiflora*), golden dalea (*Dalea aurea*), and silver-leaf evening primrose (*Oenothera macrocarpa* ssp. *incana*).

Probably the biggest problem the blackfoot daisy faces in cultivation is poor drainage and over-watering, both of which can severely shorten the life of the plant. I grew it in eastern Kansas a full 150 miles east of its native

HEIGHT	6–12 inches
WIDTH	6–12 inches
BLOOMS	May to October
SUN	Full sun
SOIL MOISTURE	Xeric once established
HARDINESS	Hardiness: USDA zones 4b–8 (up to 7,000 feet)
CULTURE	Well-drained clay, garden loam or sandy soil

range. Due to the much higher rainfall, it had to be sited on a slope, in a sand-gravel-compost soil mixture, and was never watered. Blackfoot daisy thrives with a pea gravel mulch and will gladly self-seed in the pebble substrate, but not aggressively.

The blackfoot daisy has been grown at Denver Botanic Gardens since 1984. It is relatively easy to grow from seed, or from cuttings collected late May into June, dipped in rooting hormone, and lightly misted until rooted.

Location at the Gardens: Plants can be found in the Rock Alpine Garden, the Cottonwood Border, the Laura Porter Plains Garden, and the new Desert Wash Garden.

Lotus

Nelumbo 'Mrs. Perry D. Slocum'
Nelumbonaceae

Shanelle D. Deater

By *Joe Tomocik,* Associate Director of Horticulture & Curator of Aquatic Collections, Denver Botanic Gardens

There are two species of lotus: *Nelumbo lutea,* native to North America, and *N. nucifera,* native to south-

ern Asia and Australia. Developed by famed waterlily and lotus hybridizer Perry D. Slocum, *Nelumbo* 'Mrs. Perry D. Slocum' is a hybrid between *Nelumbo lutea* and *N.* 'Rosea Plena'. *N.* 'Rosea Plena' is a double pink flowering lotus. 'Mrs. Perry D. Slocum' is now the most popular and largest selling lotus in North America.

This hardy lotus has large flowers that reach about 10 inches across. Blooming around the Fourth of July and extending through September, the flower color changes with as many as three different colors on the same plant at a given time. The flowers start out pink flushed with yellow, changing to a mix of pink and yellow the next day, followed by cream flushed with pink on the third day. The plants reach a height of 4 to 5 feet, with leaves up to 2 feet across. Though considered hardy only up to zone 6, this hybrid has been overwintered at Denver Botanic Gardens when left in undrained pools, or when covered with mulch for protection against freezing.

At the Gardens, lotuses have been displayed in our pools since 1984 or earlier. They are grown in round containers measuring 23 inches across and 9 inches deep in a

HEIGHT	25–40 inches
WIDTH	4–5 feet
BLOOMS	June to September
SUN	Full sun to part shade
SOIL MOISTURE	Aquatic, needs several feet of water
HARDINESS	Hardy in adequate depth of water (3 feet or more)
CULTURE	Responds best to heavy clay soils in five gallon or larger containers, or planted in three feet or more of water

clay-loam soil. Fertilizing is done every three weeks, inserting tablets into the soil at the rate of one per gallon of soil. Lotuses are planted beginning the first week of May.

Location at the Gardens: Lotuses are displayed throughout the Gardens' pools.

85

Desert Beargrass

Nolina microcarpa S. Watson
Dracaenaceae or Agavaceae

ILLUSTRATION BY: Linda Gerstle

Beargrass graces the garden with its arching waterfall of thin, olive-green leathery leaves during all four seasons, providing a year-round anchor for desert gardens. A member of the dragon or agave family, beargrass is native to Arizona, New Mexico, Utah, and northern Mexico, growing on steep rocky slopes of high desert grasslands, and oak or piñon-juniper woodlands.

HEIGHT	30–40-inch foliage, flowering stems from 4–8 feet tall depending on form
WIDTH	30–50 inches
BLOOMS	May to July
SUN	Full sun to partial shade
SOIL MOISTURE	Xeric once established
HARDINESS	USDA zones 4b–8 (up to 6,500 feet)
CULTURE	Well-drained clay, garden loam or sandy soil

Forming evergreen, stemless grassy clumps to 6 feet in diameter, *Nolina microcarpa* provides a bold but refined presence. The thin leaves are fibrous and leathery, with finely serrated margins. The leaves fray at the ends to create highly ornamental white curlicues that fire the imagination of artistic landscape designers. In mid- to late spring, a 5-foot-tall flower spike emerges from the rosette of foliage, covered with masses of tiny creamy-green flowers. Hardy to at least –15° F. (zone 4), beargrass thrives in full sun or part shade exposures, and requires well-drained soil.

Clean as a whistle and completely maintenance free, beargrass is perfect for nestling around water features or rain-water harvesting areas, where its grassy presence evokes riparian habitats. Or, silhouette it against a wall saturated in terracotta or saffron to highlight the wispy tips. Long-lived and tough as nails, beargrass also makes a durable container plant. More ephemeral plants nestled at the base will provide seasonal color and interest.

Early inhabitants of the Southwest used beargrass (or sacahuista) leaves to construct mats and baskets. It is still used today for weaving. Important for wildlife habitat, beargrass supplies cover for small mammals and birds. In very dry years deer and rabbits may graze on the flower stalks and leaves.

Beargrass was first grown at Denver Botanic Gardens in 1992, from seed collected in Luna County, New Mexico, with plants from numerous other sources added since that time. Panayoti Kelaidis notes that, "It has become a conspicuous and spectacular addition to our displays. *Nolina texana* is a rare native to Colorado, and *Nolina microcarpa* is well-adapted and much showier. It represents one of the many spectacular Chihuahuan and Sonoran upland plants that make such an impact in our Gardens."

Location at the Gardens:
Plants are found in Dryland Mesa, the Water-Smart Garden, and the Rock Alpine Garden.

Janet Rademacher is sales and marketing coach for Mountain States Wholesale Nursery. Judy has worked for other major southwestern wholesalers, and frequently travels the Rocky Mountain Region. She is an advocate of responsible horticulture in the frequently droughty West.

Tulip Prickly Pear

Opuntia phaeacantha Engelm.
Cactaceae

ILLUSTRATION BY: Jill Moring

By *Dominique Bayne,* Senior Horticulturist, Denver Botanic Gardens

In spring and the often intensely colored fruit in fall. They are also some of the easiest plants to grow and share. Just break off a pad and lay it on the ground in spring to see it root and thrive.

Opuntia phaeacantha, tulip prickly pear, typically has a very blue cast to the pads, which is offset by the dark brown tips of the spines. Though not as purple as some other cactus, it does have a subtle color shift through the colder months. The flowers are usually yellow with red centers and are loved by bees. This is a fairly fast-growing cactus and can reach 2 to 3 feet in height. In late summer they develop large red fruit that can persist until January or February to add yet another layer of interest during the winter.

Native to the Southwest, though scarce along the Front Range, *Opuntia phaeacantha* has become a strong favorite at Denver Botanic Gardens since its first recorded trial in 1985.

In the minds of many gardeners, the extreme low-water tolerance of prickly pears often overshadows their many other important characteristics. The term evergreen does not do them justice—many take on a purple or red tint in the winter, and few are truly green to begin with. Their distinctive shapes act as a backdrop for other xeric plants in the summer; in winter they dominate, creating snow-clad desert sculptures. Then of course there are the rose-like flowers

Location at the Gardens: It is incorporated in many different gardens including the Water-Smart Garden, Dryland Mesa, and Sacred Earth.

HEIGHT	24–36 inches
WIDTH	up to 6 feet
BLOOMS	May to June
SUN	Full Sun
SOIL MOISTURE	Dry
HARDINESS	USDA zones 4–9
CULTURE	Best in sandy or clay soil with minimal or no irrigation

Hopflower Oregano

Origanum libanoticum Boiss.
Lamiaceae

By *Angie Andrade-Foster*, Horticulturist, Denver Botanic Gardens

For twenty-seven years, *Origanum libanoticum* has graced the entrance of the Rock Alpine Garden. First planted at Denver Botanic Gardens in 1981, this plant came from a man named Ed Carman, who owned an impressive rare plant nursery in Los Gatos, California. Ed was thought to be one of the only growers of hopflower oregano during this time. Since its introduction, hopflower oregano has excelled in our Colorado gardens. *Origanum libanoticum* also has been planted *en masse* at the Waring House and the gardens along York Street. In 2004 *Origanum libanoticum* was chosen to be a Plant Select® plant because of its ability to withstand, and do extremely well with, the growing conditions of the High Plains and intermountain regions of Colorado.

As its species name suggests, *Origanum libanoticum* comes from Lebanon. Wide elevation ranges and westerly winds contribute to Lebanon's extraordinarily varied climate—much like Colorado. Hopflower oregano has a mounded growth habit, and its countless long, wiry stems hold clusters of chartreuse bracts, each decorated with small pink flowers blooming through the summer, then aging to brown and dried in the fall. *Origanum libanoticum* provides a rich flower display in full sun to part shade. It prefers well-drained loam, clay or sandy soil, and once established, will thrive on only moderate moisture.

HEIGHT	10–15 inches
WIDTH	18–24 inches
BLOOMS	May to September
SUN	Full sun to partial shade
SOIL MOISTURE	Moderate
HARDINESS	USDA zones 4b–8 (up to 7,000 feet)
CULTURE	Well-drained clay, garden loam or sandy soil

Origanum libanoticum looks best when planted along rock walls or berms, allowing the flowers to cascade and catch the eye of garden visitors.

Location at the Gardens: Plants are located in the Rock Alpine Garden, the Waring House, and the gardens along York Street.

Oriental Fountain Grass

Pennisetum orientale Rich.
Poaceae

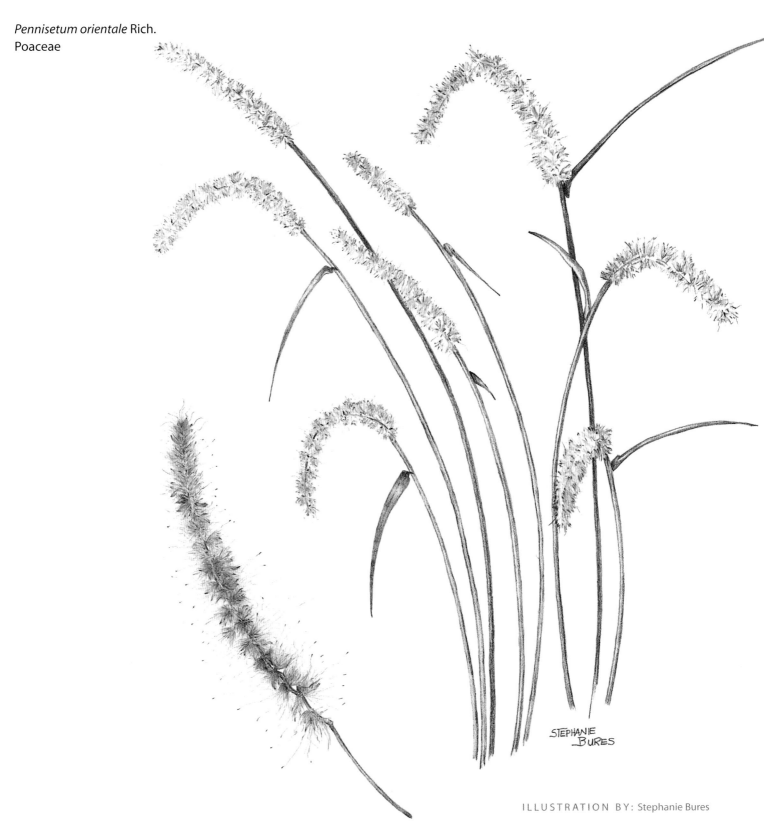

ILLUSTRATION BY: Stephanie Bures

By *Judy Sellers*

Among the many fabulous ornamental grass selections for the garden, *Pennisetum orientale* is a standout for its ease of growing, adaptability, and beauty. This native of central Asia and the Caucasus has been grown at the Gardens since 1999, a selection from the nursery of Kurt Bluemel, who is recognized as one of the earliest advocates and resources for using ornamental grasses in the landscape.

Pennisetum orientale is a dense, grayish-green clump grass that sports fuzzy, pale pink flower spikes that grow in a graceful, arching manner resembling, as its common name implies, an exuberant fountain display. "*Pennisetum*" comes from two Latin words, *penna* and *seta*, meaning feather-bristle. The soft, long-lasting spikes appear in early summer and hold into fall, gradually fading to light brown. A very versatile plant from a design perspective, it lends itself to formal plantings as seen along the El Pomar Waterway in cultivar 'Karley Rose', and the species also works well in more informal settings, as in the Romantic Gardens where it is a lovely foil for a variety of flowering perennials.

Fountain grass is extremely tolerant of various growing conditions, needing only full sun, average soil, and moderate watering. Although it can stand alone as a specimen plant, it is perhaps best displayed in groupings to get maximum effect of the flower spikes, working well in combination with broad-leaf perennials such as *Rudbeckia, Sedum* 'Herbstfreude' (Autumn Joy sedum), or *Helenium*. It

HEIGHT	24 inches, with inflorescence to 36 inches
WIDTH	24–30 inches
BLOOMS	June to September
SUN	Full sun to light shade
SOIL MOISTURE	Moderate to dry
HARDINESS	USDA zones 4b–9 (up to 7,000 feet)
CULTURE	Tolerant of most soils, does well in hot environments

is also a graceful addition to containers inter-planted with annuals such as *Verbena bonariensis* or coleus.

Although officially described in many references as hardy to zone 6 or 7, its long life at the Gardens attests to its ability to survive in colder climates as well. Our dry winters seem to enhance hardiness in many herbaceous plants—especially those of semiarid regions—by one or more zones. And, as with other ornamental grasses, it is generally left alone by deer, squirrels, and rabbits, and is impervious to insects and disease. It is a terrific plant for almost any sunny garden!

Location at the Gardens: Plants can be found in the El Pomar Waterway and in the Romantic Gardens.

Chairperson of the Gardens and Conservation Committee of Denver Botanic Gardens, **Judy Sellers** has designed gardens professionally in Colorado Springs, Colorado, and has traveled around the world studying plants and horticulture. She has published a classic book on Colorado wilderness, Colorado Wild: Preserving the Spirit and Beauty of our Land.

Foxglove Penstemon

Penstemon digitalis Nutt. Ex Sims 'Husker Red'
Plantaginaceae

By *Ross Shrigley*, Horticulturist, Denver Botanic Gardens

Penstemon digitalis is a perennial plant native to the Midwest. It grows wild from Texas to Maine in zones 3–8. The common name is foxglove penstemon, and wild varieties display white flowers with green foliage. The cultivar, 'Husker Red', is strikingly different from the common species because it delivers attractive hues of red-purple foliage. This perennial has 5-inch oblong leaves, and blooms for 2 to 3 weeks beginning in mid-June. The 1-inch long, white snapdragon-looking flowers offer a handsome contrast to the darker foliage.

HEIGHT	25–40 inches
WIDTH	12–18 inches
BLOOMS	May to July
SUN	Full sun or part shade
SOIL MOISTURE	Moderate in sun, xeric in shade
HARDINESS	USDA zones 3–8 (up to 9,000 feet)
CULTURE	Well-drained clay, garden loam or sandy soil

'Husker Red' is very easy to grow and a must-have for the no-fuss gardener, or for planting in the more water-challenged areas of the garden. Planted in full sun to part shade, seedlings hold true to the cultivar, which will quickly fill in areas if desired. The seedheads resemble large purple/chocolate drops, resting on 2-foot high stems. This plant provides fantastic three-season interest: from attractive purple rosettes in early spring, to pure white flowers in the summer, and pleasing seedheads all fall. 'Husker Red' can be utilized as a cut flower during each of these seasons.

Introduced to the green industry by Dale Lindgren, 'Husker Red' was discovered growing in a garden in Hardy, Nebraska, in 1976. After several seedling trials and selections, this plant was evaluated for the green industry in 1978 in North Platte, Nebraska. In 1985, Denver Botanic Gardens was the first botanic garden to display *P. digitalis* 'Husker Red' in the Cutting Garden. The Gardens then provided cuttings for Denver nurseries to propagate and ultimately sell in the region. 'Husker Red' proved itself to the nation when it was awarded the perennial of the year in 1996 by the Perennial Plant Association.

Location at the Gardens: Foxglove Penstemon is currently planted in Shady Lane, Birds and Bees Walk, Oak Grove, Schlessman Plaza, and the O'Fallon Perennial Border.

Pineleaf Beardtongue, Pineleaf Penstemon

Penstemon pinifolius Greene
Plantaginaceae

ILLUSTRATION BY: Michele A. Bloom

By *Ross Shrigley*, Horticulturist, Denver Botanic Gardens

Penstemon pinifolius, also known as pineleaf beardtongue, is native to the southwest states of Arizona and New Mexico. It is a wonderful semi-evergreen plant that both perennial and rock gardeners have come to enjoy. There are at least five varieties of *Penstemon pinifolius* on the market. The tubular flowers range in color from an electric red-orange in the species, to a prime sunshine yellow in cultivar 'Mersea Yellow'. There is a hybrid of these two plants that is a pleasant mango-colored variety called 'Shades of Mango'.™

The pineleaf penstemon is short in stature, with the largest varieties growing only 15 inches tall. The compact form grows only 10 inches high. *Penstemon pinifolius* is a gem of a plant that grows slowly to about 2 feet across, filling in between garden stones and nuzzling up close to sidewalks. The best view of this plant is standing several yards from it, but looking at it up close, one can see the creation of a miniature forest. The stems become woody like the soft new growth of a short shrub. Every couple of years this plant can be cut back to about 5 inches tall. This will encourage it to spread out a little further.

HEIGHT	8–15 inches
WIDTH	12–20 inches
BLOOMS	May to June with repeat bloom until frost
SUN	Full sun to partial shade
SOIL MOISTURE	Moderate to xeric
HARDINESS	USDA zones 4–8 (up to 9000 feet)
CULTURE	Well-drained garden loam, clay loam or sandy soil

The abundance of small tubular flowers creates a fiesta of color for four to six weeks in the middle of summer. It likes its roots in well-drained sandy soil or planted on sloped areas. The lower water requirements and short height make this a perfect plant for drier borders and rock gardens in full sun. Be cautious of planting low broadleaf spreading plants next to it because they will easily out-compete the penstemon, starving it of heat and sunshine. The yellow cultivars of 'Magdalena Sunshine' and 'Mersea Yellow' require a little more water than their red counterparts, but offer a complementing plant form with a different color.

The Rock Alpine Garden at Denver Botanic Gardens first displayed this plant in 1981. The West is still so young in terms of botanical discovery that this penstemon had only been found and named a few decades earlier. Denver Botanic Gardens is likely the first public garden to display the species.

Location at the Gardens: Penstemon pinifolius and its cultivars can be seen throughout the Gardens in the Birds and Bees Walk, Dryland Mesa, Yuccarama, Rock Alpine Garden, Water-Smart Garden, O'Fallon Perennial Border, and in the Romantic Garden.

Rocky Mountain Penstemon

Penstemon strictus Benth. 'Bandera'
Plantaginaceae

By *Ross Shrigley*, Horticulturist, Denver Botanic Gardens

a show-stopper. Growing wild at higher elevations (6,700 to 10,750 feet), this plant is perfect for water-smart gardens. Too much shade and moisture can make it floppy.

Penstemon strictus 'Bandera' is a cultivar that offers an especially deep purple color as it blooms heavily in June and periodically for the rest of the summer. The slender leaves are dark green and will form a tight mat 2 feet in diameter after a couple of years, making it easy to divide and share with other gardeners. *P. strictus* 'Bandera' is fragrant and beautiful in flower arrangements. One will also find the flower petals a useful dye for organic art projects. 'Bandera' is a uniform strain of the species with especially vigorous habit and tall stature. It was selected in the 1970s at the USDA Los Lunas Plant Materials Center in New Mexico and is essentially the only commonly found form of the species in cultivation. A good garden investment, 'Bandera' can live up to ten years.

Location at the Gardens: The Rock Alpine Garden first displayed *Penstemon strictus* 'Bandera' in 1980 with twenty-five specimens, and 'Bandera' is now a staple in most native garden displays. It can also be seen flowering in the Water-Smart Garden.

Visitors to the Colorado and Wyoming Rocky Mountains in June have been enjoying *Penstemon strictus* since the beginning of time. Also native to the Sangre de Cristo mountain range and Sandia Mountains in New Mexico, this 2-foot tall plant with 1-inch long, light blue to purple flowers is

HEIGHT	25–40 inches
WIDTH	12–14 inches
BLOOMS	May to July
SUN	Full sun
SOIL MOISTURE	Moderate to xeric once established
HARDINESS	USDA zones 3–8 (up to 9,000 feet)
CULTURE	Well-drained clay, garden loam or sandy soil

Desert Bluebell

Phacelia campanularia A. Gray
Hydrophyllaceae

By *Kelly D. Grummons*

That blue! That shade of blue that stops gardeners in their tracks. Rich, saturated cobalt-colored flowers demand attention much like a fine sapphire in a jeweler's case. Perhaps even more intriguing is its short stint in the garden. But, because it is a reseeding annual, the desert bluebell (*Phacelia campanularia*) will be back every May like a precious jewel you wear only on your anniversary.

Annuals, in general, are much under-appreciated in the dry land garden. As any lover of the desert knows, it is the seasonal annual flowers that paint the sands every spring or after a monsoon. In my garden, sparkling among the hardy strains of cacti and agaves are rivulets of *Phacelia campanularia, Thymophylla tenuiloba, Nierembergia hippomanica,* and other desert annuals. Over time, the seeds produced every summer or fall tend to work their way downhill, toward the bottom of each bermed garden. To keep them where you want them, collect the seeds as they ripen; then scatter them in their rightful location in November so they can germinate at will in the spring.

The desert bluebell flowers for about six weeks in May and June. The compact, mounded plants are 4 to 6 inches high and wide, and are encrusted with 1-inch-wide blue flowers from head to toe.

For a stunning color combination, sow seeds of the desert bluebell near the orange-flowered copper mallow (*Sphaeralcea coccinea*), or the scarlet blossoms of strawberry hedgehog cactus (*Echinocereus coccineus*). A combination designed by nature is the desert bluebell and the Californian poppy (*Eschscholzia californica*) with its satiny, mandarin petals.

Native to southern California, *Phacelia* performs best in lean (low levels of organic matter) soils in arid climates. It can be disappointing in wetter or irrigated gardens. Seeds sown in June will delight you with flowers in August. Sow them directly in the garden and mist lightly every day until the seedlings are half an inch high. With multiple sowings you'll have these gems in bloom from May until frost.

Location at the Gardens:

Plants can be found in Wildflower Treasures, the Rock Alpine Garden, and the Water-Smart Garden.

Co-owner of Timberline Gardens and frequent columnist in *Colorado Gardener* and other regional publications, **Kelly Grummons** has introduced a variety of ornamental plants, primarily drought-tolerant Western natives. He is a plant breeder, garden artist, and teacher, as well as a nursery jack-of-all-trades.

HEIGHT	4–6 inches
WIDTH	4–6 inches
BLOOMS	April to May, repeating to fall with successive sowings
SUN	Full sun to partial shade
SOIL MOISTURE	Xeric
HARDINESS	USDA zones 5–9 (up to 6,000 feet)
CULTURE	Well-drained garden loam, clay or sand

Alpine Phlox, Mat Phlox

Phlox condensata (A. Gray) E.E. Nelson
Polemoniaceae

By *Mark Fusco*, Senior Horticulturist, Denver Botanic Gardens

Tall garden phlox has been used in garden perennial borders for decades throughout North America and Europe. The mat-forming types, often thought of as difficult to grow, have been reserved for collectors and rock gardeners. Here at Denver Botanic Gardens we showcase large mats of *Phlox condensata* in the troughs of Wildflower Treasures, and we believe this is the way to grow this choice alpine.

Alpine phlox is native to the western United States— California, Nevada, New Mexico, Colorado, and probably Utah. In nature, in Colorado, *Phlox condensata* is almost exclusively found above tree line, occasionally growing into the open subalpine forests or on the dry open fringes of willow carrs. Windblown fellfields (rock fields) provide the primary habitat where *P. condensata* has little competition. Wind is an ally to this mat-forming phlox, which catches small particles of soil in its leaves, harvesting its own growing medium.

What sets this alpine phlox apart from others in cultivation is its prolific bloom in early April, and its longevity when planted in a trough. In Denver, where many true native alpines burn up or get leggy, *P. condensata* forms dense mats of semi-evergreen green foliage that provide year-round form. Here in Denver, a six year-old specimen will measure almost a foot in diameter in full sun.

Like most cultivated alpine plants, this one requires about one year to establish. After that, be prepared every April for a show of white to pale pink flowers spread across a tight verdant mat that every perennial gardener and collector alike will appreciate.

HEIGHT	1–3 inches
WIDTH	8–14 inches
BLOOMS	Early to mid April
SUN	Full sun to part shade
SOIL MOISTURE	Moderate to slightly dry
HARDINESS	USDA zones 2–8
CULTURE	Decomposed granite, gravel, scree, with a bit of sandy loam

Photo by Michael Kintgen

Location at the Gardens: Plants can be found in Wildflower Treasures. It also grows naturally on Mount Goliath.

Mexican Phlox, Threadleaf Phlox

Phlox mesoleuca Greene Complex
Polemonicaceae

By *Sarada Krishnan,* Director of Horticulture, Denver Botanic Gardens

Native to the Chihuahuan regions of Mexico, Southern New Mexico, and western Texas in the United States, the Mexican phloxes (*Phlox mesoleuca*) occur in shades of pink, scarlet, orange, and yellow, which are unusual in this genus. The lack of detailed study of the Mexican phloxes has led to unresolved nomenclature of this group. In addition to *P. mesoleuca,* those belonging to this complex include *P. nana, P. nana* ssp. *ensifolia,* var. *lutea* and var. *purpurea,* and various clones of hybrid origin.

The story behind the cultivation of these phloxes has a local origin. The existence of yellow-flowered *P. mesoleuca* was first documented by Cyrus Pringle in 1887, when he discovered colonies of these plants about 40 miles west of the city of Chihuahua, in northern Mexico. Paul Maslin, a retired professor of zoology, curator of the Zoological Collection at the University of Colorado at Boulder, and an enthusiastic naturalist and gardener, launched an expedition with his wife Mary to the Chihuahuan highlands in 1978 to find these yellow phloxes. After ten days of searching for the yellow phlox, the Maslins came across a large colony of scarlet phlox. The cultivar *P. mesoleuca* 'Mary Maslin' is a brilliant red-flowering selection made from this colony, which is still occasionally available in cultivation.

In addition to 'Mary Maslin', three other clones that have been commercially available from this colony include 'Tangelo', 'Denver Sunset', and 'Alborada'. On another expedition, the Gardens' own Panayoti Kelaidis joined the Maslins, and during this trip they discovered a patch of cerise-pink phlox on a steep embankment along a natural gully. These plants were highly vigorous and had larger blooms, and were named 'Arroyo', which means gully in Spanish. They probably belong to the taxon *P. purpurea.*

In nature, these phloxes flower from the start of the autumn rains in late August or early September, well into November until heavy frosts. They remain dormant during the hot and dry spring season. In Colorado, they bloom in early summer, often as early as May, and continue to flower sporadically during the hot summer months, reaching a peak in August and September, and sometimes continuing through hard frost in November. The flowers are valued for the size of their individual blossoms and their intricate markings. They grow well in deep soil with good drainage, and need regular watering and full sun.

HEIGHT	8–10 inches
WIDTH	8–15 inches
BLOOMS	May to October
SUN	Full sun to partial shade
SOIL MOISTURE	Moderate to Xeric
HARDINESS	USDA zones 5–9 (up to 6,000 feet)
CULTURE	Well-drained garden loam, clay or sand

Photo by Panayoti Kelaidis

Location at the Gardens: Currently the plants that are part of the Gardens' collections include *P. nana* var. *nana,* which dates back to 1980 and came from Paul Maslin, and *P.* 'Arroyo' dating back to 1983. Both are located in the Moraine Mound in the Rock Alpine Garden.

Cape Fuchsia

Phygelius aequalis Harv. Ex Hiern
Scrophulariaceae

By *Angie Andrade-Foster,* Horticulturist, Denver Botanic Gardens

Phygelius aequalis was first planted at the entrance of the South African Plaza in 2002. Appropriately placed, this plant can be found in its native habitat along the moist hillsides of South Africa.

Cape fuchsia is not related to the *Fuchsia* genus in spite of its common name. It is a member of the figwort family (Scrophulariaceae) to which snapdragons also belong. *Phygelius* is a very small genus of just two species. *Phygelius aequalis* and *Phygelius capensis* are very closely related and share a lot of the same characteristics. The main difference being the architecture of the inflorescence, *P. capensis* has flowers evenly spaced around the stem, whereas *P. aequalis* has flowers hanging off one side.

For a plant that is evergreen in Florida, it is surprising that *Phygelius aequalis* will survive our Colorado winters quite well. Its tall slender stems turn brown and die back to the ground at the first sign of frost, only to return lush and full the next spring.

Once the weather warms, cape fuchsia grows to about 3 feet tall, and will send underground runners to about 3 feet wide. The panicles of tubular flowers brighten the garden with red accents throughout the summer. If you look closely at the throat of the flower, it is bright yellow with red stamens and stigma protruding from the center, making the flower very attractive to pollinators.

Cape fuchsia is best grown in sun to light shade in well-draining, fertile soil, and with regular moisture. This stunning ornamental plant looks best used in a mixed border. When placed at eye-level, the drooping flowers can be seen and appreciated to their fullest.

Location at the Gardens: Plants can be found at the entrance of the South African Plaza.

HEIGHT	36–40 inches
WIDTH	30–36 inches
BLOOMS	July to September
SUN	Full sun to partial shade
SOIL MOISTURE	Moderate to moist
HARDINESS	USDA zones 5–9 (up to 6,000 feet)
CULTURE	Loam

Bell's Twinpod, Front Range Twinpod

Physaria bellii Mulligan
Brassicaceae

ILLUSTRATION BY: Michael Campbell

By *Jacalyn Raehl,* Gardener, Denver Botanic Gardens

Physaria bellii is endemic to the limestone and calcareous shales of the Niobrara formation in the northern Front Range, and also can be found on the loose shale/limestone slopes of the Pierre formation. Boulder, Larimer, El Paso, and Jefferson counties host just over twenty known populations of this species, totaling an estimated one million individual plants.

Bright yellow flowers form a halo around the grayish basal rosette of the leaves. The genus name stems from the word "physa," meaning "bubbles," in reference to its swollen seedpods, which may be seen in June, July, and August. Its common name, twinpod, also refers to the shape of the fruiting body, as it has two locules, or pods, containing seeds. There is a moderate amount of genetic diversity in *P. bellii*, as it has been known to hybridize with *Physaria vitulifera*, which grows within the same habitat. This hybridization is not considered to be a threat to *P. bellii*'s genetic identity.

Physaria bellii grows on shale outcrops within shrub communities of *Rhus trilobata* (skunkbush sumac) and

HEIGHT	4 inches
WIDTH	4 inches
BLOOMS	Early summer, fruits June–July
SUN	Full sun
SOIL MOISTURE	xeric
HARDINESS	USDA zones 4–10
CULTURE	Dry shale slopes

Cercocarpus montanus (mountain mahogany) from 5,100 to 5,750 feet in elevation. Since there is a limited habitat in which *Physaria bellii* naturally occurs, it is more sensitive to habitat destruction. Threats to the surviving populations include: mining operations (for limestone to make cement), urban sprawl, and development and introductions of invasive competitive weeds. Populations of *Physaria bellii* are estimated to be presently declining due to these factors.

Physaria bellii has been growing in cultivation at Denver Botanic Gardens since 1989 and can be seen primarily in the Endangered Species Garden, where it has been thriving on the hot, dry shale slopes. This species is certainly an asset to our local plant diversity along the Front Range.

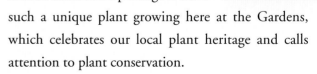

The Research Department at Denver Botanic Gardens has been conducting population studies of *Physaria bellii* since 2006. Let's hope that in another fifty years, *Physaria bellii* will be just one example of how humans can positively impact the environment with responsible consideration for the natural world around them. It is a privilege to have such a unique plant growing here at the Gardens, which celebrates our local plant heritage and calls attention to plant conservation.

Location at the Gardens: Bell's twinpod can be observed growing in the Endangered Species Garden, Wildflower Treasures, Plains Garden, Dryland Mesa, and on the Green Roof.

Limber Pine

Pinus flexilis James 'Damfino'
Pinaceae

By *Jerry Morris*

P.T. Barnum knew. The largest and smallest things are fascinating to people. Be it the world's largest ball of string or a tiny cell phone/media player/computer that fits in the palm of your hand, we love the unusual. That holds true in the gardening world as well, from the towering redwoods to dwarf conifers that barely reach knee height.

Dwarf conifers start life as a mutated bud, or stem, on a normal tree or shrub. This mutation, known as a Hexen-Besen, results in a dense cluster of shoots forming on an abnormally short length of stem. It gives the appearance of a broom on a branch; from this we get the common term, witches' broom. While a witches' broom can be caused by a wide variety of organisms ranging from insects to viruses, in conifers these "brooms" typically form due to a genetic abnormality. The brooms are collected and grafted onto rootstalk to create new dwarf conifers. To retain the dwarf properties, the plants are propagated by cuttings or seed to build a stock for sale.

The witches' broom that was to become *Pinus flexilis* 'Damfino' was found when a friend and I were hunting elk in North Park, Colorado. I looked up into a very large, old limber pine to see a witches' broom and commented that it was a very good broom. My friend asked, "When you collect it, what will you name it?" I replied, "Damned if I know!"

Usually, when one collects and grows a broom, it needs to be named before it is introduced into the trade. A common way to identify it is to name it after something close by, such as a town or ranch, or after a person, or for an outstanding physical characteristic. Trying to think of a name for this newly found treasure, I remembered there was a nice creek nearby and thought about naming it after the creek. But when asked the new name, I answered, "Damfino!"

Since this hunting excursion in 1960, *Pinus* 'Damfino' has been introduced into the nursery trade and is now sold across the United States, as well as in Europe. The needles are a good green, and growth is usually described as having a flat top. It has an upright growth habit, growing half as wide as it is tall. A slow grower, it typically grows only 1 to 2 inches per year.

HEIGHT	2–4 feet after many years
WIDTH	2–3 feet
BLOOMS	Insignificant, in spring
SUN	Full sun to part shade
SOIL MOISTURE	Moderate to slightly dry
HARDINESS	USDA zones 3–8
CULTURE	Loam, sandy or gravely soil, or well-drained clay

Location at the Gardens: (Editor's Note) Denver Botanic Gardens is fortunate to have an extensive collection of dwarf conifers, many donated by renowned plantsman Jerry Morris. The Dwarf Conifer Berm garden showcases the many varieties of these miniatures. Others are incorporated among the plantings throughout the garden. The small limber pine, *Pinus flexilis* 'Damfino' is among the favorites in the collection.

Jerry Morris, long-time owner of Rocky Mountain Tree Care, retired decades ago in order to explore for unusual forms of conifers in the West. He has introduced over 1,000 unique selections of witches' brooms and mutations of western conifers.

Ponderosa Pine

Pinus ponderosa P. Lawson & C. Lawson
Pinaceae

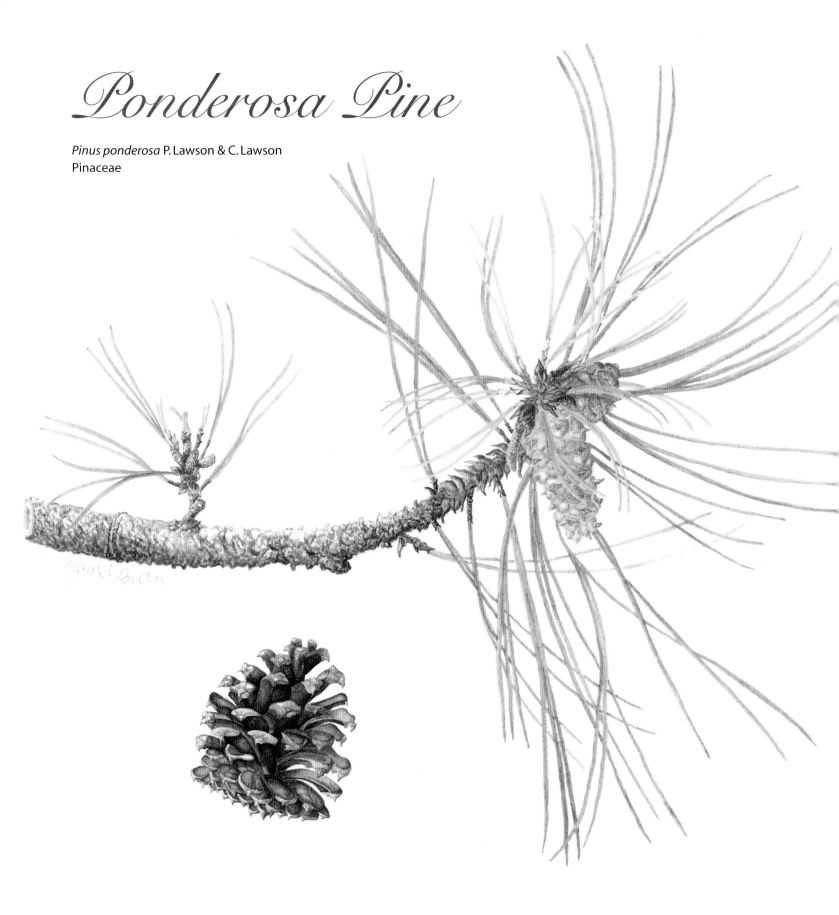

ILLUSTRATION BY: Joan Brennan

By *Dr. Anna Sher*, Director of Research & Herbaria, Denver Botanic Gardens

Dr. Sher thanks Ebi Kondo, Senior Horticulturist at Denver Botanic Gardens, for his contributions to this chapter.

Ponderosa pines are native to the western and central United States, western Canada, and northern Mexico. This species is highly drought and wind tolerant, is long-lived, and can grow to 60 to 90 feet tall and 30 to 40 feet wide. The needles are 3 to 5 inches long, and grow in bundles of 2 to 4 (usually 3). It is evergreen, with needles lasting three to four years, and the major needle drop is in September and October. The bark begins very dark, turning reddish-brown to orange-yellow around ninety years of age. They are an excellent choice for supporting wildlife, as the seeds are a choice food for several species of native birds, chipmunks, and squirrels, and the needles are eaten by blue and spruce grouses.

Denver Botanic Gardens is the first (and perhaps only) garden to use native ponderosa pines in its Japanese Garden, Shofu-En. The characteristic, gnarled trees in Japanese gardening, called *niwaki*, are usually achieved through careful pruning over many years, inspired by those seen growing on rocky outcrops that were trained by wind and snow. However, the trees in Shofu-En (meaning "Garden of Pine and Wind") are not simulations, but were shaped naturally over four-hundred years on the exposed cliffs in the foothills of the Colorado Rocky Mountains. Local volunteers donated 130 such pines for this garden, designed by Dr. Koichi Kawana, and first trained by Kai Kawahara, a true pioneer in this unusual approach. The pines in this garden thus represent a unique mixture of East and West, by using native western trees to create a signature Eastern-style garden. As such, they are among the oldest *niwaki* trees anywhere in the world, rivaled only by the most ancient gardens in Japan.

Our ponderosa pines are also represented in the Gates Montane Garden, where they are in their more recognizable tall and straight form. This shape is expected in forests on more sheltered mountainsides. However, it should be understood that the very different morphologies found in the two gardens are both "natural," reflecting the incredible diversity that can be created by environment alone.

As a native tree, ponderosa pines are fairly carefree, tolerating both irrigated and dry environments, although it is important not to over-water or over-fertilize. Saplings should be planted in the spring. Pruning is not essential, but can be done in spring and summer. To create the Japanese "character," new growth (called candles) is selectively pinched to inhibit growth in the spring, and in summer, needling can be done to allow light in and encourage lateral growth.

HEIGHT	60–90 feet
WIDTH	30–40 feet
BLOOMS	Inconspicuous in May
SUN	Full sun to partial shade
SOIL MOISTURE	Moderate to xeric
HARDINESS	USDA zones 4b–8 (up to 8,000 feet)
CULTURE	Well-drained garden loam or sandy soil

Location at the Gardens: They have been grown at the Gardens since 1979 and are in the Japanese Garden (Shofu-En) and the Gates Montane Garden.

Encyclia Orchid

Prosthechea mariae (Ames) W.E. Higgins
Synonyms: *Encyclia mariae* (Ames) Hoehne,
Euchile mariae (Ames) Withner
Orchidaceae

ILLUSTRATION BY: Annie Reiser

By *Nick Snakenberg,* Associate Director of Horticulture & Curator of Orchids and Tropical Collections, Denver Botanic Gardens

Orchids are visitor favorites at many botanic gardens and have been a part of Denver Botanic Gardens' collections since the 1960s. Long-time supporters Bill and Micki Thurston have a keen interest in orchids and have made many expeditions south of the United States' border to study these plants in their native habitat. As a result of their early interest and support, some of the first orchids to form the foundation of Denver Botanic Gardens' orchid collection were species from Mexico and Central America.

Prosthechea mariae is a small epiphytic orchid native to high elevations in northeast Mexico. Though small in stature, it produces surprisingly large flowers—up to 4 inches in size—in early to mid-summer. It prefers intermediate to cool growing conditions, with medium to high light, and plenty of humidity. As an epiphyte, it grows best mounted on a small limb or a cork bark slab rather than in a pot.

Our specimen has been in the collection since 1998, and in 2005 the Gardens received a Highly Commended Certificate from the American Orchid Society in recognition of the plant's superior form, size, and color. This distinction is marked by the addition of the clonal name 'Denver Botanic Gardens' to this specimen's proper name.

HEIGHT	5–8 inches
WIDTH	6–10 inches
BLOOMS	Early to mid-summer
SUN	Full sun to partial shade
SOIL MOISTURE	Moderate
HARDINESS	Tender indoor plant for greenhouse or sunroom culture
CULTURE	Best mounted on cork bark or other epiphytic medium

Photo by John Stewart

Location at the Gardens: Like most of Denver Botanic Gardens' orchid collection, this plant is not on permanent display, but is only brought from our behind-the-scenes collection greenhouses when there are blossoms for visitors to enjoy.

Buckley's Oak

Quercus buckleyi Nixon & Dorr
Fagaceae

By *Jacalyn Raehl,* Gardener, Denver Botanic Gardens

Buckley's Oak is native to central and north-central Texas, southern Oklahoma, and Kansas. Trees can be found growing on rocky limestone ridges and slopes, and alongside small creeks and streams. In its native habitat, it thrives in the higher elevations.

The species name *buckleyi* is in honor of American geologist and botanist S.B. Buckley, who served as a State of Texas geologist in the mid-1800s.

Quercus buckleyi provides a stunning red fall color display, and its show continues long after other leaves have already fallen. The tree grows to 50 feet tall on average, but it has been known to grow up to 75 feet in height.

This deciduous tree has an incredible tolerance to hot, dry weather that is common in Denver throughout the summertime. *Quercus buckleyi* is relatively low-maintenance compared to others because it is best when left unpruned. Its acorns provide a valuable source of food for wildlife, such as squirrels, birds, and deer. Since it is native to alkaline soils, it thrives in the soils found in Denver. *Quercus buckleyi* does best in full sun on well-drained soils.

In addition to its impressive fall color display, the newly emerging leaves of Buckley's oak often have a hint of a reddish hue in the spring.

Location at the Gardens: *Quercus buckleyi* can be found growing in Dryland Mesa and the Oak Grove gardens.

HEIGHT	70 feet
WIDTH	60 feet
BLOOMS	Spring
SUN	full sun
SOIL MOISTURE	Moisture: low
HARDINESS	USDA zones 5–9
CULTURE	well-drained alkaline soil

Gambel Oak

Quercus gambelii Nutt.
Fagaceae

By *Sarada Krishnan,* Director of Horticulture, Denver Botanic Gardens

Native to the Rocky Mountain region, from Wyoming south to Mexico and west to Nevada, Gambel oak is a small tree or large shrub usually under 20 feet in the wild. It belongs to the beech family (Fagaceae), and is also called scrub oak. In Colorado, it is common in the lower montane and foothills west of the Continental Divide, and from Denver southward on the eastern slope. The name honors the nineteenth-century western plant collector, William Gambel.

HEIGHT	6–20 feet
WIDTH	6–10 feet
BLOOMS	Inconspicuous in May
SUN	Full sun to partial shade
SOIL MOISTURE	Moderate to xeric once established
HARDINESS	USDA zones 4b–8 (up to 7,000 feet)
CULTURE	Well-drained garden loam

The Gambel oak plays a significant role in our ecosystem by providing food and other services to wildlife and humans. The state insect, the Colorado hairstreak butterfly (*Hypaurotis crysalus*), depends on the Gambel oak, which is the only source of food for its caterpillars. Ethnobotanical significance includes the use of various parts of this plant for numerous purposes by Native Americans. Acorns were a very important source of protein food for early southwestern tribes. Beams of oak were used in roof construction. At various archaeological sites, numerous oak implements—bows, arrows, scoops, handles, hoes, and snowshoes—have been excavated. The Navajos used Gambel oak as an ingredient to dye wool.

There are twenty-two accessions of Gambel oak recorded in the Gardens' plant collections database. The oldest one recorded dates back to 1978, and is located in the Woodland Mosaic. In 1979, more Gambel oaks were planted in the Gates Montane Garden. One specimen, at the north end of that garden, towers well over 40 feet tall, rivaling the lushest specimens one could encounter in the wild. It likely dates to the time the Gates Montane Garden was first planted by Saco DeBoer, the first garden at York Street, exactly fifty years ago.

The Gambel oak is easy to grow. It likes full sun and is extremely drought tolerant. Branching occurs near the ground, but it can be pruned to develop a tree form. Ornamentally, Gambel oaks are grown mainly for their foliage, which provides spectacular color in the fall.

Location at the Gardens: These plants are distributed in many gardens with specimens in the Gates Montane Garden, Water-Smart Garden, Dryland Mesa, Ponderosa Border, Oak Grove, and Woodland Mosaic.

Shumard's Oak

Quercus shumardii Buckley
Fagaceae

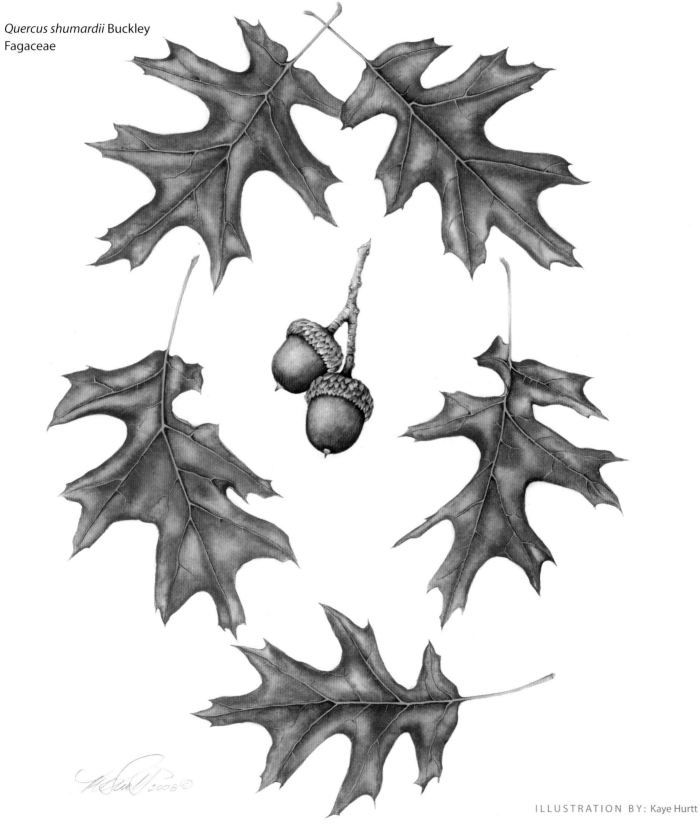

ILLUSTRATION BY: Kaye Hurtt

By *Alan M. Schroder*, Conservatory Horticulturist, Denver Botanic Gardens

The *Quercus shumardii* at the site of the Waring House and garden here at Denver Botanic Gardens is a specimen that has withstood the true test of time. In fact, this Shumard's oak is Colorado's state champion specimen, meaning it is the largest Shumard's oak in Colorado. Considering the age and size of this specimen, Denver Botanic Gardens values this oak almost more than any other oak on site. In fact, this is the largest of the oak trees here at the Gardens. It's hard to miss this tree as one passes by the gardens because of its vast size and sheer strength. At first glance, it may be hard for one to guess its age, but very few people know that it's over one hundred years old and 96 feet tall.

Quercus shumardii, or Shumard's oak, is found in the plant family Fagaceae, the beech family. Shumard's oak is a native to the United States and has a distribution range including the Atlantic and Gulf coastal plains from North Carolina to northern Florida and west into central Texas, growing in zones 4b–8. Shumard's oak can grow to 80 feet tall and more, with a spread of up to 60 feet wide, making for a magnificent specimen if it reaches its full size.

This tree has an oval to round growth habit filling in great over time. Shumard's oak is a dioecious perennial that flowers anywhere from March to April and into May with inconspicuous female flowers and somewhat larger drooping male catkins. Like most oaks, this oak will hybridize freely with other oaks if given the chance. Shumard's oak is valued for commercial use mostly as a shade tree but it also serves as a food source and shelter spot for many types of birds and small mammals.

Quercus shumardii grows best in full sun, but as it ages it can tolerate partial shade. A well-drained soil that receives regular moisture will help accelerate this tree's growth, although it appears to be somewhat drought tolerant as it ages. Unlike the similar red and pin oaks that are more frequently sold locally, Shumard's oak seems to thrive on alkaline soils. With a wonderful red to golden-brown fall color in late October lasting into November, and its ability to be a wonderful shade tree, *Quercus shumardii* is a must have for oak enthusiasts and plant buffs alike.

Location at the Gardens: The tree can be seen at the Waring House and garden.

HEIGHT	40–80 feet (Denver Botanic Gardens' specimen is off the charts!)
WIDTH	40–60 feet
BLOOMS	Inconspicuous in spring; acorns in fall
SUN	Full sun to partial shade
SOIL MOISTURE	Moderate
HARDINESS	USDA zones 4b–8 (up to 6,500 feet)
CULTURE	Well-drained garden loam, clay loam or sandy soil

Waterlily

Rocky Mountain Legacy Collection
Nymphaea Cultivars

ILLUSTRATION BY: Susan T. Fisher
N. 'Denver's Delight'

By *Joe Tomocik,* Associate Director of Horticulture & Curator of Aquatic Collections, Denver Botanic Gardens

The Rocky Mountain Legacy Collection (RMLC) is a collection of eight unique, outstanding, beautiful waterlilies created during the twenty-eight-year tenure of Denver Botanic Gardens' water gardens curator, Joseph V. Tomocik. As part of our waterlily trials and working with leading hybridizers and nurseries, waterlilies were evaluated, named, and introduced. The eight cultivars constituting the RMLC are: *N.* 'Attorney Elrod', *N.* 'Colorado', *N.* 'Cynthia Ann', *N.* 'Denver', *N.* 'Denver's Delight', *N.* 'Joey Tomocik', *N.* 'Stan Skinger', and *N.* 'William McLane'.

N. 'Attorney Elrod': This tiny rose-colored hardy waterlily persisted in the Gardens' collections for over twenty years before receiving its name.

N. 'Colorado': The first salmon-colored waterlily, it was introduced exclusively by Lilypons Water Gardens. This is a hardy waterlily.

N. 'Cynthia Ann': A prolific producer of small peach flowers, this hardy waterlily was spotted by Bruce McLane in the Gardens' pools and was then propagated by Florida Aquatic Nurseries for the waterlily trade.

N. 'Denver': This hardy waterlily produces French vanilla-colored flowers.

N. 'Denver's Delight': This is a selection of a waterlily that has grown in nearby Berkeley Lake for over fifty-five years. This hardy waterlily is the first to flower each season and is a delightful pink color. It was named by Gardens' supporter Carol Purdy.

N. 'Joey Tomocik': Named for Joe Tomocik's daughter, this hardy cultivar is considered to be the brightest yellow waterlily.

N. 'Stan Skinger': This tropical waterlily is a heavy bloomer producing small apricot-colored flowers and has rich variegated leaves that darken with age.

N. 'William McLane': Another tropical waterlily, it produces vivid purple flowers and won the Banksian Award as best overall new waterlily in 1997.

Photo by Joe Tomocik

Location at the Gardens: The Rocky Mountain Legacy Collection waterlilies are displayed throughout the Gardens' pools.

HEIGHT	5 inches
WIDTH	4 feet
BLOOMS	June to September
SUN	Full sun to part shade
SOIL MOISTURE	Aquatic, needs several feet of water
HARDINESS	Hardy in adequate depth of water (3 feet or more)
CULTURE	Responds best to heavy, clay soils in 5-gallon or larger containers, or planted in 3 feet or more of water

123

'Linda Campbell' Rose

Rosa 'Linda Campbell'
Rosaceae

ILLUSTRATION BY: Constance Sayas

By *Joan Franson*

What an incredible rose 'Linda Campbell' is. Here is a hybrid rugosa rose that was hybridized by Ralph S. Moore and introduced in 1991. Ralph is most famous for his stellar work in miniatures and in shrub and old garden roses. He crossed a miniature rose with a hybrid perpetual rose to create the beautiful 'Linda Campbell' rose. This shrub rose has large, dark green rugosa foliage (leaflets with a wrinkled rather than smooth surface), which is semi-glossy. The flowers are medium sized individually, but come in clusters of five to twenty blooms with a quick repeat. The red in this rose is a clear medium red, with no trace of the bluing or magenta tones of red that are most often seen in the species of old garden and shrub roses of yesterday. This red has yellow in its breeding background and that brings out the clear full saturation of red, as seen in the modern hybrid teas and floribundas.

This rose has a local connection to Colorado and the Denver area. Linda Campbell was a dear friend, and her talents and abilities naturally brought her to local, as well as national, prominence in the world of roses. Linda loved all roses but especially the miniatures. When I first met her in 1972, it was instantly clear that she was a rare talent. She became a rose-show judge and a consulting rosarian; frequently she also was an exhibitor in rose shows. At the national level in the American Rose Society, her deep interest and thorough follow through gained her many friends.

HEIGHT	4–6 feet
WIDTH	3–5 feet
BLOOMS	May to September
SUN	Full sun to partial shade
SOIL MOISTURE	Moderate
HARDINESS	USDA zones 4b–8 (up to 7,000 feet)
CULTURE	Well-drained garden loam

Among them was the rose hybridizer Ralph Moore. How fitting it is that Ralph used a miniature rose in the creation of 'Linda Campbell'.

Her husband, Dr. Bill Campbell, was a long-time supporter of, and consultant to, Denver Botanic Gardens. He served for many years on the Gardens' Board of Trustees, was frequently on the horticulture committee, and was always available for advice in the entire Gardens. Bill also started his own rose nursery, High Country Roses, which is still run by his daughter in Utah. His independent research into roses led to his deep understanding of rose history and propagation.

This is a hardy shrub that gets along with minimal care and can reach 5 feet or so. It needs to be planted in well-drained soil in a location with six or more hours of sunlight. As a versatile shrub, it can be placed in the landscape in a number of ways. 'Linda Campbell' will be an attraction as a specimen shrub featured separately by a garden gate; as an entrance signal by a walkway to welcome all; tucked into a mixed perennial border where it shines with other reds and yellows; or as a joyful friend in your favorite place to sit and view your garden.

Location at the Gardens: Several 'Linda Campbell' roses were planted in the xeriscape gardens at Centennial Garden, as well as two in the rose garden at York Street. There is also a lovely display of several bushes planted around the Linda Campbell gazebo in the War Memorial Garden in Littleton, Colorado.

Joan Franson is a regional authority on shrub roses and leader of the American Rose Society, Federation of Garden Clubs, and the Colorado Garden and Home Show. She has gardened in Arvada for many decades, and has been a volunteer at Denver Botanic Gardens for much of its history.

Balkan
Salvia

Salvia ringens Sibth. & Sm.
Lamiaceae

By *Mike Kintgen,* Horticulturist, Denver Botanic Gardens

Forget the bright red annual *Salvia splendens* or deep bluish-purple *Salvia* x *sylvestris* 'Mainacht' and instead picture a graceful lavender-blue perennial salvia whose blooms dance on airy stems 4 feet above attractive leaves. Add a bloom time that lasts from early June to August, good drought tolerance, no signs of pest or disease, and one has a plant destined to be a block buster.

Salvia ringens is rather an unknown salvia that is native to Greece. Like so many of the Turkish *Salvia,* it much prefers Denver's semi-arid climate to the moist and gentle climate of the British Isles, which may explain why it's rarely seen in gardens there. Seed can be hard to come by as well. All of our plants in the Rock Alpine Garden were propagated as cuttings, and are likely identical clones that rarely set seed.

Stock of *S. ringens* in all Denver area gardens probably dates from a collection that Jim Archibald of the United Kingdom made in Greece in the late 1970s or early 1980s. Denver Botanic Gardens first acquired the plant in 1982 as seeds from Jim's seed catalog. Unfortunately the plants did not stick around, but thanks to Panayoti Kelaidis who kept the plant going in his own garden, we were able to reacquire plants in 2002. Since that time it has thrived in the Upper Meadow of the Rock Alpine Garden in almost pure Denver clay, with some added gravel and around five to six deep soakings per year. Six years later the plants continue to get better and better.

HEIGHT	3–4 feet (more if it is moist spring)
WIDTH	2–3 feet after 6 years (clump forming)
BLOOMS	Early June to August
SUN	Full sun to very light shade (may flop if in too much shade)
SOIL MOISTURE	Rather xeric if grown in un-amended clay (will flop or rot with too much water)
HARDINESS	Safely to Zone 5 (zone 4 or possibly even colder) (probably up to 7,000 feet)
CULTURE	Clay, loam or sand as long as it is not wet.

Salvia ringens is just one of the stellar long-lived and generally xeric salvias native to Greece and Turkey. Some others grown at Denver Botanic Gardens include *Salvia cyanescens, Salvia pisidica,* and *Salvia recognita.*

Salvia ringens would look lovely combined with all kinds of xeric plants, such as yellow-orange *Eremurus* or sulfur-yellow *Eriogonum umbellatum,* both of which enjoy similar conditions. Or it could be a lovely addition to some of the more drought tolerant shrub roses. Since this particular salvia is not yet widely grown, only guidelines can be given on its true hardiness and elevation range. It has been rock hardy in Denver for over two decades. Hopefully, as it becomes more available, people will have the opportunity to try one of the most spectacular hardy salvias.

Location at the Gardens: Plants can be found in the Upper Meadow of the Rock Alpine Garden.

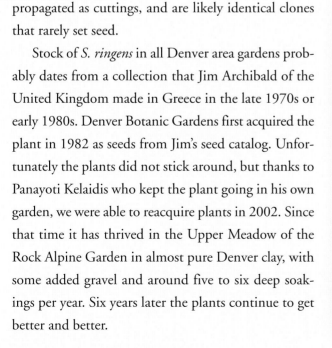

Little Bluestem

Schizachyrium scoparium (Michx.) Nash
Poaceae

Little bluestem is native to North America and is widely distributed throughout the United States. Originally planted in the Plains Garden in 1983, *Schizachyrium scoparium* was chosen because it is native to the plains regions of Colorado. This bunch grass has become a reliable favorite for its terrific bronze/red fall color and adaptability to drought. Although it is showcased in most of our native plant gardens, little bluestem is also used in many other gardens to add texture and interest in the winter months.

Little bluestem is a common component in revegetation projects, as it can grow in a variety of soil types and growing conditions. However, it is best adapted to growing in medium to dry infertile soils in full sun. Its drought tolerance is an important characteristic for its use in Denver as an accent plant in borders or natural prairies.

Little bluestem has green-blue blades of grass throughout the summer, and the entire plant turns deep burgundy-red after the first frost. It is best left alone throughout the winter because it retains its beautiful reddish hue throughout the season. Cut it back in early spring for robust growth in summer.

This warm-season grass provides shelter for small mammals and songbirds. The seeds are also eaten by a variety of birds. *Schizachyrium scoparium* is an important forage plant for livestock, deer, and elk as well. Several cultivars are available for a variety in color and forage value.

Native American plains tribes utilized this plant in a variety of ways. The Comanche used bundles of stems in their spiritual "sweat lodge" ceremonies. *Schizachyrium scoparium* has also been harvested by the Comanche for medicinal purposes. The Lakota tribe softened the grass and lined their moccasins with it to serve as insulation in the winter.

Location at the Gardens: *Schizachyrium scoparium* can be found throughout the Gardens, but most notably within the Western Panoramas, the Plains Garden, the Ornamental Grasses Garden, and Sacred Earth.

HEIGHT	18 inches to 3 feet at maturity (varies with soil type and moisture)
WIDTH	1.5 feet
BLOOMS	Fall
SUN	Full sun
SOIL MOISTURE	Low
HARDINESS	USDA zones 3–9
CULTURE	well-drained, medium to dry infertile soil

Redbirds
in a Tree

Scrophularia macrantha Greene ex Stiefelhagen
Scrophulariaceae

ILLUSTRATION BY: Gai Swanson

By *Maria Bumgarner,* Horticulturist, Denver Botanic Gardens

Photo by Panayoti Kelaidis

Scrophularia macrantha is the aphrodisiac in the plant collector's world. It is highly sought after for its gorgeous tubular red flowers and lustrous dark green foliage. David Salman, president of Santa Fe Greenhouse and High Country Gardens, gave it the common name "redbirds in a tree," which accurately describes how the little red flowers resemble a profile of a red bird with a white beak. It is related to *Penstemon,* however, it is completely unique. It can grow more than 36 inches tall and a foot or more wide with an informal habit.

In the wild it is a very rare species endemic to New Mexico. Panayoti Kelaidis collected a few seed capsules at 7,200 feet on his first ascent of Cooke's Peak in Luna County, New Mexico. Imagine the journey those few capsules have taken from 7,200 feet to become a successful plant in the Rock Alpine Garden. In addition, the plant developed into a 1997 introduction with High Country Gardens and was recently promoted by Plant Select® in 2008. Besides having a fascinating history, this plant succeeded in a variety of soils, is drought tolerant, and blooms July through October.

Scrophularia macrantha is valuable in wildlife habitats because it is only pollinated by hummingbirds, which highly prize its nectar. In addition to great color and unique wildlife benefits, this plant also has the ability to intertwine with neighboring plants for support. It would be a great addition to a fence, mixed with a vine near an arbor, or as a naturalized planting.

Location at the Gardens: Scrophularia macrantha can be found in Wildflower Treasures and the Water-Smart Garden.

HEIGHT	30–50 inches
WIDTH	15–25 inches
BLOOMS	July to October
SUN	Full sun to partial shade
SOIL MOISTURE	Moderate to lightly irrigated xeriscape
HARDINESS	USDA zones 4b–8 (up to 7,000 feet)
CULTURE	Well-drained clay, garden loam or sandy soil

Stiff Greenthread, Navajo Tea

Thelesperma filifolium (Hook.) A. Gray
Asteraceae

ILLUSTRATION BY: Hannah Rottman

By *Michael Bone*, Senior Horticulturist, Greenhouse and Propagation, Denver Botanic Gardens

As my early interest in horticulture evolved into the study of more native and dry-loving plants for the garden, one of my first treasures found was *T. filifolium*. I was hiking on the backside of North Table Mountain and I saw a hillside loaded with bright yellow daisies. At that point I was convinced that I was seeing a *Coreopsis verticillata*, but did not yet know much about Colorado's native flora. I ended up growing thousands of *Coreopsis* thinking that I was growing my greenthread and producing native plants for the landscape.

HEIGHT	12–18 inches
WIDTH	8–18 inches
BLOOMS	May to September
SUN	Full sun to partial shade
SOIL MOISTURE	Xeric once established
HARDINESS	USDA zones 4–9 (up to 8,000 feet)
CULTURE	Well-drained clay, garden loam or sandy soil

After a while, I became suspect as I would see the *Coreopsis* fry in our dry summers and the plants on the hill would always look beautiful. Upon researching the plant, I found that what I was seeing was a *Thelesperma*. I have since learned that the population I was seeing on North Table Mountain was in fact *T. ambiguum*, a local gem of a plant that is very similar to *T. filifolium*. Both are great garden plants. *T. filifolium* is about 1½ feet tall and equally wide, and it is covered for most of the summer with perfect golden yellow daisies and fine thread-like foliage.

T. filifolium is common in dry areas up and down the low elevations of the Rockies, and can be found blooming with cacti and other dry-loving wildflowers. A tough, beautiful alternative to the wet-loving *Coreopsis verticillata*, greenthread is a great example of how one can use a local plant to replace water loving exotics. The feel of many garden styles can be replicated—Japanese gardens, lush English perennial borders—while still using a native plant palette.

The Navajo made a tea from the foliage that reportedly had a soothing and calming effect. I get that same feeling just watching this plant grace my garden and dot the hillsides around my home and stomping grounds.

Location at the Gardens: Plants can be found in all of our native gardens and the Water-Smart Garden.

Victoria Waterlily

Victoria 'Longwood Hybrid'
Nymphaeaceae

By *Joe Tomocik,* Associate Director of Horticulture & Curator of Aquatic Collections, Denver Botanic Gardens, and *Sarada Krishnan,* Director of Horticulture, Denver Botanic Gardens

The *Victoria* 'Longwood Hybrid' is a cross between *V. cruziana* and *V. amazonica.* In its native habitat, *V. amazonica* grows along the Amazon Basin in South America and *V. cruziana* is native to Paraguay, Bolivia, and Argentina. Developed at Longwood Gardens by hybridizer Patrick Nutt in 1961, the Longwood Hybrid is the first successful cross between these two species. Possessing the best attributes of both parents, this plant has been displayed and cultivated at the Gardens each year since 1984. It is a main attraction during the months of August and September.

First discovered by Bohemian botanist and naturalist Tadeáš Haenke in 1801 during an exploration trip to the Amazon Basin in the Mamoré River, the Victoria waterlily is known for its giant platter-like leaves. Named for Queen Victoria, this plant was brought to bloom in cultivation almost fifty years later in England. The undersides of the leaves are covered in long, sharp spines. Its intricate vein structure is a structural engineering marvel, and has served as an inspiration for the architectural design of Victorian-era glass conservatories.

At Denver Botanic Gardens, the Victoria waterlily, a warm-season plant, is planted around mid-July each season to ensure that it is not subjected to cold damage. It is planted in a clay-loam soil in containers measuring 23 inches wide and 9 inches deep. Smaller containers will produce somewhat smaller plants. Aquatic plant fertilizer is applied on a weekly basis to maintain the health of the plants.

Leaf diameter varies from year to year, reaching about 50 inches during optimal years. Flowers can reach a diameter of 10 inches. First flowering also varies from year to year, with flowers appearing as early as late June to as late as early September. Being non-hardy in Denver, these plants are grown from seeds each year by the Victoria Conservancy. (The Victoria Conservancy is a nonprofit foundation operated by Trey and Nancy Styler of Greenwood Village, Colorado, which provides Victoria waterlilies to over one hundred public gardens around the world. The Stylers grow both *V. amazonica* and *V. cruziana* under highly controlled conditions to produce seed and plants of both species and hybrids on an annual basis.)

HEIGHT	10 inches
WIDTH	8–10 inches
BLOOMS	July to September (depending on how early they are put out)
SUN	Full sun
SOIL MOISTURE	Aquatic, needs three feet or more water depth
HARDINESS	Tender, must be planted out only in warmer months
CULTURE	Needs warmer water temperatures and attentive care. Responds to classic aquatic plant culture (heavy soil, fertilization)

Location at the Gardens: This plant is displayed in the Upper (Victoria) Pool and Monet Pool.

Eve's Needle, Faxon's Yucca

Yucca faxoniana (Trel.) Sarg.
Agavaceae

ILLUSTRATION BY: Susan Lyons

By *Dan Johnson*, Associate Director of Horticulture & Curator of Native Plants, Denver Botanic Gardens

For contrast, this is one of the giants of the yucca world. In its native haunts in the Big Bend region of Texas and south into Mexico, it can create spiky forests on sandy sun-drenched plains, but is seen just as often perched on rocky mountainsides in otherwise lunar landscapes. It tolerates unimaginable heat and drought. As with most yuccas, it matures slowly, with old dry leaves relaxing flat against the trunk. This thatch likely provides some protection against extremes of heat and cold, and is a common feature of most arborescent yuccas. The trunk is substantial, easily reaching 14 inches or more in diameter, and up to 30 feet tall, with a massive crown of leaves reminiscent of true palms.

The massive clusters of flowers emerge in late spring, sometimes nestled among the leaves, sometimes rising just above the crown. For sheer size and drama, there are few plants that will rival this one in the garden.

HEIGHT	10–20 feet (taller in habitat)
WIDTH	8–12 feet
BLOOMS	June
SUN	Full sun
SOIL MOISTURE	Xeric once established
HARDINESS	USDA zones 5–9 (up to 6,000 feet in urban settings)
CULTURE	Well-drained clay, garden loam or sandy soil

Y. faxoniana have been grown for many decades in New Mexico as far north as Santa Fe, sometimes suffering from cold there in severe winters, but usually resprouting from the base. So far we have not experienced any damage, but a well-drained, sunny, sheltered microclimate will certainly suit them best.

Though common in many locations, even in Colorado, these were hardly cultivated in gardens prior to our plantings in the early 1980s. They have since become a favorite subject for rock gardens and native landscapes throughout the West.

Location at the Gardens: Plants can be found in Yuccarama and the Dryland Mesa.

Spanish Bayonet, Harriman's Yucca, Dollhouse Yucca

Yucca harrimaniae Trel.
Agavaceae

ILLUSTRATION BY: Heidi A. Snyder

By *Dan Johnson,* Associate Director of Horticulture & Curator of Native Plants, Denver Botanic Gardens

Y. harrimaniae originated in the United States and is commonly found in an irregular swath from far western Oklahoma west to central Nevada. Plants were initially collected by Panayoti Kelaidis and Allan Taylor for the Rock Alpine Garden, and have been at Denver Botanic Gardens since 1980.

HEIGHT	10–20 inches
WIDTH	8–14 inches
BLOOMS	May and June
SUN	Full sun
SOIL MOISTURE	Xeric once established
HARDINESS	USDA zones 4–9 (up to 8,000 feet in urban settings)
CULTURE	Well-drained clay, garden loam or sandy soil

There is room in every sunny garden for this gem. Among the smallest of all yuccas, typical specimens have a dense crown of leaves just 12 to 14 inches across. Very tiny forms have been found in several Utah locations. In habitat, some of these have small rosettes of leaves just 3 to 5 inches across, evoking the words "cute," "sweet," and "precious"—not descrip-

tors usually associated with yuccas! In some forms, they will even have a short trunk, resembling miniature Joshua trees.

Leaves are very narrow and rich green, with silvery white edges that fray into long curled filaments, lending a furry glow to the symmetrical rosettes. These characteristics vary quite a bit among different forms, but all are exquisite and long lived in a dry well-drained garden.

Flowers are a typically creamy white, and stand on tall stems from 1 to 3 feet above the crowns. Placed among large boulders and short grasses, the effect is sublime. Miniature western landscapes are at your fingertips with this *sweet* little yucca!

Location at the Gardens: Plants can be found in the Rock Alpine Garden, Dryland Mesa, Water-Smart Garden, and Yuccarama.

Beaked Yucca

Yucca rostrata Engelm. Ex Trel.
Agavaceae

ILLUSTRATION BY: Patricia Greenberg

By *Dan Johnson,* Associate Director of Horticulture & Curator of Native Plants, Denver Botanic Gardens

are flexible with a slight twist, and seem to shimmer in the sun as they catch the slightest breeze. The crowns have nearly perfect symmetry, and often remain un-branched, or sparingly so.

Y. rostrata flowers a bit later than *Y. thompsoniana,* usually in June, and it seems to bloom less often as well. The flower stalks we have observed have been shorter and broader than Thompson's, though still raised a bit above the leaves. Flowers are a brighter white as well, but all this is anecdotal, based on just a few years' experience, as we've only had the Beaked yucca at the Gardens since 2000. There is certainly variation as many yuccas will easily hybridize, and superior selections are already being made in the industry.

Regardless of the quibbles among taxonomists, the Thompson's yucca and Beaked yucca, as offered in nurseries, do seem distinct. As container-grown plants become more available, I expect to see many a dry garden transformed. Each has its merits—in fact, I think a garden without several of each will be the poorer for it!

Location at the Gardens: Yucca rostrata can be found in Yuccarama and the Water-Smart Garden.

Yucca rostrata **has been called** the queen of yuccas, and it is our good fortune that it seems to thrive here! If I could have just one large yucca, this would be it. Contrasting with *Y. thompsoniana* (shown on the next page), the *Y. rostrata* forms that are available commercially have longer leaves, usually colored a silvery blue-green with a fine golden edge. The leaves

HEIGHT	8–12 feet (taller in habitat)
WIDTH	4–6 feet
BLOOMS	June
SUN	Full sun
SOIL MOISTURE	Xeric once established
HARDINESS	USDA zones 5–9 (up to 6,000 feet in urban settings)
CULTURE	Well-drained clay, garden loam or sandy soil

Thompson's Yucca

Yucca thompsoniana Trel.
Agavaceae

By *Dan Johnson*, Associate Director of Horticulture & Curator of Native Plants, Denver Botanic Gardens

Thompson's yucca, and the Beaked yucca (*Yucca rostrata*) that is shown on page 140, are seen by some to be one species, and others believe they are distinct. Still others believe that *Y. thompsoniana* is a northern variant of *Y. rostrata*. Both yuccas originated in the United States and Mexico, and are found in the Big Bend region in Texas. Having seen them both in their native habitat in the Big Bend, I can understand the confusion, as there seems to be a gradation of forms and characteristics, and populations do seem randomly mixed in some areas. For my part, I am not a taxonomist, but I do see differences in the variously labeled forms found in cultivation.

Yucca thompsoniana seems to be among the hardiest of the tree-type yuccas, which we have grown at Denver Botanic Gardens since 1998. Its proportions are more modest than some, even fitting into a small garden with striking results. The rigid sharp-tipped leaves range from bluish to olive green with the finest golden edge—an especially attractive feature when backlit by morning or evening sun. Flowering stalks rise with amazing speed in May, and the creamy pendulous flowers are lifted as much as 4 or 5 feet above the leaves. As with all yuccas, its own particular species of Pronuba moth must be present for pollination, so seed pods are rarely produced in cultivation away from its native habitat.

This yucca will branch readily, especially after flowering. Trunks can be 12 inches across, and up to 8 feet or taller. A planting of these is a delight all year, especially in the depths of winter when the many leafy crowns stand bright green, capped with freshly fallen snow.

HEIGHT	10–15 feet (taller in habitat)
WIDTH	6–8 feet
BLOOMS	June
SUN	Full sun
SOIL MOISTURE	Xeric once established
HARDINESS	USDA zones 5–9 (up to 6,000 feet in urban settings)
CULTURE	Well-drained clay, garden loam or sandy soil

Location at the Gardens: Yucca thompsoniana can be found in Yuccarama, Dryland Mesa, and the Water-Smart Garden.

143

Photo Credits

For Historical Highlights

(in order of appearance, thus not chronological order in all instances)

1943: Logos by Claude Hansen

1944: Horticulture House. Denver Botanic Gardens Photo Collection

1941: Mrs. Kalmbach. Denver Botanic Gardens Photo Collection

1949: Mrs. Evans. Denver Botanic Gardens Photo Collection

1951: Dr. Shubert. Denver Botanic Gardens Photo Collection

1952: City Park Gardens with building. Denver Botanic Gardens Photo Collection

1952: City Park Gardens, gardeners. Denver Botanic Gardens Photo Collection

1957: Mt. Goliath. Photograph by Albert E. Daraghy

1958: Field of York Street site. Photograph by Jack Fason

1959: Waring House and truck. Photograph by C. M. Stafford

Cemetery pictures in order, top down:

Courtesy of Denver Public Library, Western History Collection, Z-304

Courtesy of Colorado Historical Society, Denver Post Historic Collection, Scan #10036473

Courtesy of Denver Public Library, Western History Collection, X-29384

Courtesy of Denver Public Library, Western History Collection, M-1501

Courtesy of Denver Public Library, Western History Collection, X-29388

1960: Long and Wilmore. Denver Botanic Gardens Photo Collection

1959: A. Hildreth. Denver Botanic Gardens Photo Collection

1964: Conservatory. Denver Botanic Gardens Photo Collection

1962: H. Zeiner. Denver Botanic Gardens Photo Collection

1965: E. Bibee. Denver Botanic Gardens Photo Collection

1966: Plaque. Photograph by Bill & Berta Anderson

1970: W. Gambill and P. Kelaidis. Courtesy of Merle M. Moore

1968: J. C. Mitchell. Denver Botanic Gardens Photo Collection

1971: S. Gignac. Photograph by Susan Praetz-Fay

1973: Barns at Chatfield. Denver Botanic Gardens Photo Collection

1973: Covered Wagon Frieze. Denver Botanic Gardens Photo Collection

1976: Krohn House. Photograph by Bill & Berta Anderson

1974: A. Garrey. Denver Botanic Gardens Photo Collection

1975: Ruth P. Waring. Denver Botanic Gardens Photo Collection

1975: Plains Garden marker. Denver Botanic Gardens Photo Collection

1977: K. Kawana. Courtesy of Merle M. Moore

1978: Japanese lantern. Denver Botanic Gardens Photo Collection

1978: Tea House dedication. Denver Botanic Gardens Photo Collection

1978: Rock Alpine Garden. Denver Botanic Gardens Photo Collection

1981: M. Honnen. Photograph by Bill & Berta Anderson

1981: Pavilion. Photograph by Bill & Berta Anderson

1979: Dedication. Courtesy of Robert Dodge.

1980: Summer concert. Denver Botanic Gardens Photo Collection

1984: Tiffany china. Denver Botanic Gardens Photo Collection

1985: Blossoms of Light. Denver Botanic Gardens Photo Collection

1986: Ed Connors. Denver Botanic Gardens Photo Collection

1989: Pumpkin Festival. Denver Botanic Gardens Photo Collection

1989: Deer Creek Schoolhouse. Denver Botanic Gardens Photo Collection

1995: P. Kelaidis. Denver Botanic Gardens Photo Collection

1998: Romantic Gardens. Denver Botanic Gardens Photo Collection

1993: Water-Smart Garden. Denver Botanic Gardens Photo Collection

1997: O'Fallon Perennial Border. Photograph by Albert E. Daraghy

1997: A. O. Dowden. Photographer unknown. Anne O. Dowden Collection, Denver Botanic Gardens

1999: Drop Dead Red Border. Denver Botanic Gardens Photo Collection

2001: Education Building. Denver Botanic Gardens Photo Collection

2001: Interiorscaping. Denver Botanic Gardens Photo Collection

2003: Cloud Forest Tree. Denver Botanic Gardens Photo Collection

2000: Centennial Gardens. Denver Botanic Gardens Photo Collection

2000: SCFD. Denver Botanic Gardens Photo Collection

2003: PlantAsia. Denver Botanic Gardens Photo Collection

2004: Sensory Garden. Denver Botanic Gardens Photo Collection

2003: Dos Chappell. Denver Botanic Gardens Photo Collection

2007: Native Plant Garden. Courtesy of Barbara Baldwin

2008: Bond initiative. Denver Botanic Gardens Photo Collection

2007: Brian Vogt. Denver Botanic Gardens Photo Collection

2007: Green roof. Denver Botanic Gardens Photo Collection

For Early Visionaries

George W. Kelly: Painting by O. Miniclier

Michiel Walter Pesman and daughter: Denver Botanic Gardens Photo Collection

Ruth Porter Waring: Photographer unknown. J. Morley Collection, Denver Botanic Gardens

Saco Rienk DeBoer: Courtesy of Denver Public Library, Western History Collection, F39349

Plant Index

Alpine Columbine
(*Aquilegia saximontana*).......24

Alpine Phlox
(*Phlox condensate*)...........102

American Hornbeam
(*Carpinus caroliniana*) 32

Ashy silktassel
(*Garrya flavescens*) 54

Balkan Salvia
(*Salvia ringens*) 126

Beaked Yucca
(*Yucca rostrata*) 140

Bell's Twinpod
(*Physaria bellii*)...............108

Blackberry Lily
(*Belamcanda chinensis*)........30

Blackfoot Daisy (*Melampodium leucanthum*) 82

Buckley's Oak
(*Quercus buckleyi*)............116

Cape Fuchsia
(*Phygelius aequalis*)..........106

Clown Fig (*Ficus aspera*)........52

Curly-Leaf Mountain Mahogany (*Cercocarpus ledifolius*) 34

Cutleaf Fleabane
(*Eriogonum compositus*) 48

Daphne (*Daphne* x
transatlantica)..................40

Desert Beargrass
(*Nolina microcarpa*) 86

Desert Bluebell
(*Phacelia campanularia*).....100

Dollhouse Yucca
(*Yucca harrimaniae*)..........138

Dotted Gayfeather
(*Liatris punctata*) 74

Encyclia Orchid
(*Prosthechea mariae*) 114

Eve's Needle
(*Yucca faxoniana*) 136

Faxon's Yucca
(*Yucca faxoniana*) 136

Fendler's Hedgehog Cactus
(*Echinocereus fendleri*)........46

Foxglove Penstemon
(*Penstemon digitalis*)...........94

Frémont's Barberry
(*Mahonia fremontii*)...........76

Front Range Twinpod
(*Physaria bellii*)...............108

Gambel Oak
(*Quercus gambeli*) 118

Greenleaf Manzanita
(*Arctostaphylos patula*)........28

Hairy Clematis
(*Clematis hirsutissima*) 38

Hardy Gazania
(*Gazania linearis*)..............57

Harriman's Yucca
(*Yucca harrimaniae*)..........138

Hopflower Oregano
(*Origanum libanoticum*)......90

Limber Pine (*Pinus flexilis*)...110

'Linda Campbell' Rose
(*Rosa* 'Linda Campbell') 124

Little Bluestem (*Schizachyrium scoparium*) 128

Little Walnut
(*Juglans microcarpa*)...........66

Lotus (*Nelumbo*).................84

Mat Phlox (*Phlox condensate*) .102

Mexican Phlox
(*Phlox mesoleuca*).............104

Navajo Tea
(*Thelesperma filifolium*) 132

Orange Sneezeweed
(*Hymenoxys hoopesii*) 61

Oriental Fountain Grass
(*Pennisetum orientale*).........92

Owl's-Claws
(*Hymenoxys hoopesii*) 61

Pineleaf Beardtongue
(*Penstemon pinifolius*) 96

Pineleaf Penstemon
(*Penstemon pinifolius*) 96

Pine-mat Manzanita
(*Arctostaphylos nevadensis*) 26

Plains Blackfoot (*Melampodium
leucanthum*) 82

Ponderosa Pine
(*Pinus ponderosa*).............112

Purple Hardy Ice Plant
(*Delosperma cooperi*)..........42

Red Barberry
(*Mahonia haematocarpa*)......78

Red Flowered False Yucca
(*Hesperaloe parviflora*).........59

Red Yucca
(*Hesperaloe parviflora*).........59

Redbirds in a Tree
(*Scrophularia macrantha*)....130

Rock Clematis
(*Clematis Columbiana*)........36

Rock Daisy (*Melampodium
leucanthum*) 82

Rocky Mountain Penstemon
(*Penstemon strictus*) 98

Roundleaf Horehound
(*Marrubium rotundifolium*) ..80

Shumard's Oak
(*Quercus shumardii*)..........120

Snakeroot (*Liatris punctata*) ...74

Spanish Bayonet
(*Yucca harrimaniae*)..........138

Stiff Greenthread
(*Thelesperma filifolium*) 132

Sulphur Flower (*Eriogonum
umbellatum*)....................50

Tall Bearded Iris (*Iris*)..........63

Texas Red Yucca
(*Hesperaloe parviflora*).........59

Thompson's Yucca
(*Yucca thompsoniana*)........142

Threadleaf Phlox
(*Phlox mesoleuca*).............104

Torch Lily
(*Kniphofia caulescens*) 68

Torch Lily (*Kniphofia
triangularis*) 71

Tulip Prickly Pear
(*Opuntia phaeacantha*)........88

Victoria Waterlily (*Victoria*) .134

Waterlily (Rocky Mountain
Legacy Collection)...........122

Yellow Hardy Ice Plant
(*Delosperma nubigenum*)......44